"I gathered up my courage and wrote to some well-known Americans, explaining that I wanted to compile a 'from-the-heart collection of the feelings we've always wanted to share with our fathers—from the most whimsical to the straightforward and serious,' and inviting them to contribute letters as long or as short as they liked. I wasn't at all sure how many answers I would get (if any!) or what they would be like—and I certainly didn't anticipate the kind of enthusiasm and generosity which actually came about."

From the introduction
by L. Norma Cox

DEAR DAD

Edited by L. Norma Cox

BALLANTINE BOOKS • NEW YORK

I don't know the meaning behind the song she sang...
Perhaps the song was simply a lullaby that she remembered
from many years ago, and the father was hope and love
and desire, and a belief in miracles...

John Pielmeier, *Agnes of God*

Dear Dads, everywhere...
This collection is about you and for you,
the fathers we loved and tried to love.

And, to let you know that for all the
things we did say, attempted to say, or
ever wanted to say—in expressing our
thoughts and love—many have tried
before us and many, many more will try
after us.

Gratefully,
LNC

SPECIAL THANKS

My heartfelt gratitude to my dear, dear parents, Frank and Lillian Cox for giving me a lifetime of love and for standing by me all these years as I followed a path through life that took so many interesting turns. And to my son and good friend, Robert A. Olmsted—thank you for your enthusiasm *and* love *and* sense of humor as I completed *Dear Dad*.

I am grateful to Joan Fortgang for her loyalty to this project and the work and energy she so willingly put into it. I wish to thank Karen Pokross, Charlotta Woodley, Florence and Danny Gabler, for their personal support—and Vine Phoenix, Caryl Liberman, Hilary Hamann, Lorene Allen, Linda Casey, Marlin Fitzwater, Ingrid Vanderstok, Sally Guenzer, Lee Ray, Madeline Kelly, Marlene Franks, Linda Arney, Melinda Gilliam, Thelma Elkjer and Joan Edwards for their many courtesies. I am most grateful to Dr. Pat Howell and Nathan Mitchell of Saybrook for their encouragement and patience when I needed it most. I am particularly indebted to Cynthia Giles for her special insights; to Rachel Bolton and Hallmark Cards, Inc., for so generously sharing their research information with me; and to Tim Murari and Richard Soll for giving of their time.

I am especially grateful to Dr. Joseph F. Lagana for his input and steadfast care; to George Berkowitz for his great wisdom, strength, counsel and wit; and to all the men and women who contributed letters to this book—and in doing so gave so much of themselves.

CONTENTS

PART I:
"DEAR DAD . . ."
LETTERS AND PHOTOS

PART II:
THOUGHTS ABOUT FATHERS

INTRODUCTION

A year ago, I gathered up my courage and wrote to some well-known Americans, explaining that I wanted to compile a "from-the-heart collection of the feelings we've always wanted to share with our fathers—from the most whimsical to the straightforward and serious," and inviting them to contribute letters as long or as short as they liked. I wasn't at all sure how many answers I would get (if any!) or what they would be like—and I certainly didn't anticipate the kind of enthusiasm and generosity which actually came about.

When the first letters began to arrive, I was amazed at their candor, and at the love which filled every page. There were no "pretty" letters, superficial and syrupy; and there weren't any letters which focused more on the famous writer than on Dad. Every response I received was open and heartfelt and unpretentious. And as the process of bringing this book together has unfolded, the contributors have continued to be wonderfully cooperative. The result has been one of the nicest "work" experiences anyone could ask for.

Another result has been the validation of an opinion I have held for a long time: there are a lot of beautiful fathers out there, and a lot of sons and daughters who love them. Fathers have had some very bad press in this century; experts of all kinds have told us that the American father is too distant, too protective, too busy, too weak, too authoritarian—too *something*. But I knew that my own father was one of the most important and positive influences in my whole life, and I thought there must be some more like him around.

I also realized, however, that even for those of us who know how lucky we are to have the fathers we have, it's still difficult to express that feeling to the man himself. Partly, it's just that the opportunity never seems to arise. So I had the idea of giving people a chance to share their feelings of love and gratitude (and yes, sometimes sadness) not only with their fathers, but with all the other grown-up children who are looking for a way to say "I love you, Dad." And that was the beginning of this book.

Of course, it's not just lack of opportunity that makes it hard to talk to our fathers; it's also a lot of other factors, some of them built into the society we live in. Traditionally, Mom has been portrayed as the nurturer, the listener, the emotional center of the family; Dad has always been off at work, gone to war, or hidden behind the newspaper. One indication of how far the national scales have been tipped in Mom's favor is the fact that we've had an official Mother's Day for seventy-three years—and an official *Father's* Day for only fifteen! That's right. It's only been fifteen years since President Nixon signed a congressional resolution establishing Father's Day as a national holiday. Although Father's Day had been celebrated in an unofficial way since 1916, there was a curious resistance to giving Fathers the same official status as Mothers.

Senator Margaret Chase Smith tried to persuade Congress to even things up in 1957. When that didn't work, she tried to shame them into it, with a strongly worded statement: "As far as I can gather, it seems that the Congress has been guilty now for forty years of the worst possible oversight, to say the least, perpetrated against the gallant fathers, young and old, of our land . . . Either we honor both parents, mother and father, or let us desist from honoring either one. But to single out one of our two parents and omit the other is the most grievous insult imaginable."

Even though Senator Smith's point seems obvious today, it didn't sway the congress; they still refused to give Fathers their Day. I wonder if perhaps the male members of Congress found it hard to acknowledge their feelings for their fathers; or maybe, since they were mostly fathers themselves, after all, they were uncomfortable with the idea of being the *object* of a lot of expressed feelings. (How often do we hear Dad saying "Now don't make a fuss over me"?) But whatever the reasons, their resistance continued until 1972.

Father's Day still runs a distant second to Mother's Day in such measurements as cards bought and flowers sent, but it's firmly a part of our national life now, and it's an occasion which gives us a chance to break through the emotional barriers and the traditional structures that can make it difficult to reach our fathers. Many of us—*and* our fathers—have been victims of the stereotyping that made Dad the strong, silent provider, the authority figure, the distant parent; we imagined he didn't want or need expressions of affection and appreciation, while he imagined he *shouldn't* want these things. And often, the result has been an awkward silence where there might have been a moment of closeness.

It's never too late, though, to try again to break that silence. And perhaps the letters in *Dear Dad* can help. For one thing, they offer company. Looking through the letters in this book brings home the depth of our feelings about our fathers, and reveals both the diversity of people's relationships with their fathers, and the similarities. None of these writers says the same thing, and yet there are themes that run through the letters and through each of our own lives; there are stories and phrases and observations which reach out and remind us of our own feelings, our own memories; and there are portraits of many different kinds of fathers, no two alike, but each vividly recalled for all he did and all he was to the child who loved him. The incompletions are here too, and the losses and the sorrows that are part of all human life. Some of the letters are to fathers long dead, some to fathers never quite known. Some evoke the poignancy of growing up, growing apart, growing old. But these notes of sadness, like those of joy, reveal the strength of love.

The letters in this book are very real. A few were actually written and sent to the fathers many years ago; most were written especially for *Dear Dad*. But all are marked with a directness and eloquence which comes not from writing skill (none of the contributors are professional writers) but from the heart. The book includes every letter I received, not just the "good ones," and none have been edited or changed in any way. I wish I could have reproduced the letters just as they were sent to me, but the truth is, many would be just too hard to read. Most of the contributors either wrote their letters by hand or did the typing themselves, which added to the very personal character of the letters, but also made some passages difficult to decipher.

I was almost too timid to ask the contributors for pictures of their fathers, but I finally did, and again, their response was enthusiastic. Quite a few of them hunted up old family pictures and entrusted me with the original snapshots; more than one contributor wrote something like "this is the only picture I have of me with my father—*please* take care of it and return it soon." (In a few cases, there were no pictures at all, and in a few others, no pictures which could be adequately reproduced in the book.)

This willingness on the part of the contributors—every one extremely successful and very busy—to give of themselves and their time has continually surprised and touched me. I chose to invite these particular people (as well as many others who couldn't participate for personal reasons, or because of time constraints) into the book for several reasons. They are from a wide variety of backgrounds and represent diverse opinions. And they are people who will be remembered as having made lasting impressions on our lives, through their careers in politics, sports, business, and the arts. Perhaps most important, they are people who have kept their dignity and humor and personal integrity, in spite of the many difficulties of public life.

But I think the special efforts of all the contributors represent more than the fact that they are nice people. I think it's also a testament to the importance of fathers and the pleasures of remembered love.

My hope for *Dear Dad* is that it will offer us all some starting points and a little inspiration for thinking about the things we never quite found the words or the opportunity to say to our fathers. Some very special people have opened their hearts and shown us what *they* want to say to *their* fathers. Now it's our turn.

LNC

ACKNOWLEDGMENTS

Grateful acknowledgment is made to the following for permission to quote from copyrighted material:

The lines from *Agnes of God* appear courtesy of John Pielmeier.

Houghton Mifflin Company, for the passage from *Into Eternity: The Life of James Jones, American Writer*, by Frank MacShane. Copyright © 1985 by Frank MacShane. Reprinted by permission of Houghton Mifflin Company. Also for the passage from *Home Before Dark*, by Susan Cheever. Copyright © by Susan Cheever. Reprinted by permission of Houghton Mifflin Company.

Curtis Publishing Company, for the passage from *The Autobiography of Eleanor Roosevelt*. Copyright © 1937, 1949, 1958, 1960, 1961, by Anna Eleanor Roosevelt.

A.S. Barnes and Company, Inc., for the passage from *Mark Twain at Your Fingertips*, edited by Caroline Thomas Harnsberger.

Basic Books, Inc., for the passage from *The Life and Letters of Charles Darwin*, edited by Francis Darwin. Copyright © 1959, by Basic Books, Inc. Reprinted by permission of Basic Books, Inc.

Mr. Howard Morhaim, and St. Martin's Press, for the passage from *Dark Star: The Untold Story of the Meteoric Rise and Fall of the Legendary John Gilbert*, by Leatrice Gilbert Fountain with John R. Maxim. Copyright © 1985 by Leatrice Gilbert Fountain and John R. Maxim.

The New Yorker, for the passage from "Profiles, Governor Mario Cuomo," by Ken Auletta. Reprinted by permission; © 1984 by Ken Auletta. Originally in *The New Yorker*.

Harper and Row, Publishers, Inc., for the passage from *Letters of E.B. White*, pages 388–389, collected and edited by Dorothy Lobrano Guth. Copyright © 1976 by E.B. White. Reprinted by permission of Harper and Row, Publishers, Inc. Also for the passage from "Finding the Father," from *Selected Poems*, by Robert Bly. Copyright © 1977, by Robert Bly. Reprinted by permission of Harper and Row, Publishers, Inc. Also for the excerpt from *With Malice Toward None: The Life of Abraham Lincoln*, by Stephen B. Oates. Copyright © 1977, by Stephen B. Oates. Reprinted by permission of Harper and Row, Publishers, Inc.

Weybright and Talley, Inc., for the passage from *Shaw, An Autobiography*, edited by Stanley Weintraub. Copyright © 1969, by The Trustees of the British Museum, The Governors and Guardians and the National Gallery of Ireland, and The Royal Academy. Introduction and editorial matter, copyright © 1969, by Stanley Weintraub.

Viking Penguin, Inc., for the passage from *Journal of a Novel: The East of Eden Letters*, by John Steinbeck. Copyright © 1969, by the Executors of the Estate of John Steinbeck. Reprinted by permission of Viking Penguin, Inc. Also for the passage from *Selected Letters of James Joyce*, edited by Richard Ellmann. Copyright © 1957, 1966, by The Viking Press, Inc. Copyright © 1966, 1975, by F. Lionel Monro as Administrator of the Estate of James Joyce. Reprinted by permission of Viking Penguin, Inc.

Random House, Inc., for the passage from *One Christmas*, by Truman Capote. Copyright © 1982, 1983, by Truman Capote. Reprinted by permission of Random House, Inc. Also for the passage from *Freud: The Man and the Cause*, by Ronald W. Clark. Copyright © 1980, by E.M. Partners, A.G. Reprinted by permission of Random House, Inc. Also for the passage from *Swanson on Swanson*, by Gloria Swanson. Copyright © 1980, by Gloria Way, Inc. Reprinted by permission of Random House, Inc.

Miss Elizabeth Stevens, Curtis Brown, for the passage from *Robert Louis Stevenson*, by James Pope Hennessey. Copyright © 1974, by Sir John Pope Hennessy. Published in the U.S.A. by Simon and Schuster, Inc.

Simon and Schuster, Inc., for the passage from *Frank and Maisie: A Memoir with Parents*, by Wilfrid Sheed. Copyright © 1985, by Wilfrid Sheed. Reprinted by permission of Simon and Schuster, Inc.

The John Day Company, for the passage from *Pearl S. Buck: A Biography*, by Theodore F. Harris. Copyright © 1969 by The John Day Company, Inc.

Macmillan Publishing Company, for the passage from *Lemmon*, by Don Widener. Copyright © 1975, by Donald Widener. Reprinted with permission of Macmillan Publishing Company.

Ms. Shirley Collier, Shirley Collier Agency, for the passage from *Miners Hill*, by Michael O'Malley.

Charles Scribners' Sons, for the passage from "Fathers and Sons," in *Winner Take Nothing*, by Ernest Hemingway. Copyright © 1933, Charles Scribners' Sons; copyright © renewed 1961, Mary Hemingway. Reprinted with the permission of Charles Scribners' Sons.

PART
ONE

Richard Adler

You probably remember—as I do—Richard Adler's great hit songs, many of which have become standards in the repertories of the top vocalists of our time, tunes like "Hey There," "Hernando's Hideaway," "Whatever Lola Wants," "Heart," "Everybody Loves a Lover," "Steam Heat." It's no exaggeration to say that his songs have changed and enchanced the way we all listen to the world.

Remember his *Pajama Game* and *Damn Yankees*? He got a Tony Award and then was honored with an Emmy Award for one of his ballets. His *Yellowstone* Overture, which premiered in Carnegie Hall was nominated for a Pulitzer Prize—as was his *Wilderness* Suite.

A native New Yorker, born to Clarence and Elsa Adler, Richard has served as a consultant on entertainment to Presidents Kennedy and Johnson.

Richard Adler—an early riser—wrote his letter for the book at 5 A.M. one morning! He was in his study at his home in Southampton and was searching for something he had dropped under the sofa, when he found my letter I had written to him five months earlier, and sat down immediately to write the following to his father. The photo is of Richard.

Dear Dad,

I remember you so well as a brilliant chamber music pianist and a teacher considered to be of enormous dimension and so able to show others, of all ages (and I mean from five to eighty-five), how to make the piano "sing."

When I was a small boy, many times I used to hear you shouting phrasing instructions to your pupils heightening the beauty of the phrase . . . "hold the note longer . . . break the tempo to accentuate that most beautiful expression of feeling Mr. Chopin created for us . . . build the glissando on the fourth, fifth and sixth beats to give it the drama it is supposed to have . . . allow the half measure rest to feel like a half measure . . . like taking a deep breath . . . don't let that ritard feel like a freight train one hundred cars long passing over a railroad crossing!"

Listening to those instructions while I was doing my homework evidently made a deep impression on me (and at the time, if anything, I resented the interruptions. My concentration in my early youth was far from perfect.)

Today, I realize that when I am rehearsing a musical with the principals or chorus or both, I try to make the lyrics sound like an extension of the dialogue that precedes them. My notes to the singers sound strangely familiar, echoing the past with ghostly reverberations. The same applies in my dialogues with conductors who are rehearsing (or interpreting my classical orchestral work). "That is a half measure rest . . . no longer than taking a deep breath . . . please maestro, don't let that ritard feel like a freight train one hundred cars long passing over a railroad crossing!"

Love,
Richard

Tracy Austin

Tracy Austin began playing tennis at the tender age of two, and went on to become, at sixteen, the youngest player ever to win the U.S. Open Championship. She did this, incredibly, by defeating Martina Navratilova in the semi's and Chris Evert-Lloyd in the finals! In September of 1981, at Flushing Meadows, New York, millions of tennis fans saw her outlast Wimbledon winner Navratilova to capture her *second* U.S. Open crown. Tracy's remarkably consistent record enabled her to become the youngest player in history to earn a million dollars in prize money—and to receive the world's No. 1 tennis ranking.

You may have seen her successful television acting debut in the "Mork and Mindy" show. Guest appearances on the "Merv Griffin Show" and "Late Night with David Letterman" are also part of Tracy's off-court activities. She was born to George and Jeanne Austin in Rolling Hills, California. Her entire family is a great source of support, in part because brothers John and Jeff—as well as sister Pam—have all played tennis professionally. This typical photo, on the next page, shows Tracy on the courts.

January 29, 1985

Dear Dad:

Thank you for spending so much of your free time with me. Although you had a demanding job and five kids, we always felt you were behind us in every way.

I remember you helping me with my homework, especially when I started to travel. You were always patient and willing to help me catch up when I didn't understand something I had missed. I am so glad you stressed the importance of a good education because I'm grateful for it now.

I recall you driving us to tennis tournaments on the weekends, and making sure we had the attitude of just doing the best we could. Also, I had a lot of fun when you took my friends and me to the park or horseback riding on Sundays. You and I had a terrific time when we would take long bike rides.

Dad, I want you to know you have been a very good influence and model in shaping my morals and values as a person. Thank you for being such a loving father.

I love you,
Tracy

Kaye Ballard

Kaye Ballard landed on the cover of *Life* after her starring role in the Broadway musical *The Golden Apple*. The hit television show "The Mothers-in-Law," made her a household name.

Her odyssey into show-biz began as a teenager in Cleveland, Ohio, where she had been born to Vincent and Lena Ballota. One day the rambunctious Kaye announced to her startled conservative Italian family that she was going to be a star. Kaye toured the vaudeville circuit with Spike Jones, then with Vaughn Monroe and later with Stan Kenton. Moving to New York, she was cast in the highly successful *Three to Make Ready*, then moved to London in *Touch and Go*. She has also found time to record several albums and to play in many of the country's most prestigious clubs.

Kaye presently lives in New York's Upper East Side and, I learned, is the proud owner of three uncut, apricot French poodles: Pockets, Punky and Shirley. What a wonderful picture those poodles make on the sidewalks of New York! The genial gentleman in the following photograph is her father Vincent. The dramatic lady is Kaye.

Dearest Pop,

I appreciate your instilling in my brain that a deal is a deal. And I'm very proud to have lived by that creed. What you instilled in my *heart* is sometimes more difficult for me to live up to—courage, tolerance, patience, faith. But I keep on trying and I always will, because I want you to be as proud of me as I am of you.

All the very best of my love to the very best of all fathers,

Your Kaye

Bill Beutel

Bill Beutel is almost like a member of my family. This is also true for most New Yorkers—and for countless others across the U.S. For more than 20 years, he has nurtured—and been nurtured by—the human approach taken by WABC-TV's "Eyewitness News." A pioneer on that program, Bill remains a vital member of the Channel 7 (WABC) news team, as well a correspondent for its highly praised public service program, "Crime Stoppers."

As anchor at WABC-TV he wrote and produced an Emmy Award winning documentary, "Don Xoai: The Town the Viet Cong Couldn't Kill," and subsequently won five other Emmys for various documentaries. His 1981 documentary, "Made in Japan," an examination of Japanese industry and culture, has become a primer for many American corporations. For several years, beginning in 1968, Beutel served as ABC News London Bureau Chief, a position that earned him, as he puts it—"a sort of Ph.D. in journalism." While in London, he covered the aftermath of the Six-Day War (1968) in the Middle East and the Civil War in Nigeria.

The son of William and Stella Beutel, Bill was

born in Osceola, Indiana. The photo on the next page of him as a boy with his dad, is an especially precious family memento. Young Bill is in the middle.

July 21, 1986

Dear Dad,

   You left us 25 years ago. I remember it as if it were
yesterday. I was working in New York, and I got a call
from an old friend in Cleveland. I thought it was to be
just a social call, but it wasn't. I cried, and as I left the
office, Maggie said she was sorry. I said, so was I,
because he was a hell of a good guy. It was April 12,
of 1962. And the newspapers never let me forget the
date, even if I wanted to, because it was just 17 years
from the day FDR died, and every April 12, someone
writes that FDR died on this day in 1945.

   Maggie was a writer at CBS, and I've often
wondered why I remember her comment to me, and
mine to her, so clearly. I've never found a really good
answer to that question, and I have a feeling I don't
need one. Enough that I remember what I said to her:
"He was a hell of a good guy."

   Ask me what I remember specifically of your life,
and I have a hard time. I guess we played ball together,
a little bit. Not as much as some of the other guys and
their fathers. We used to go hunting, and shooting,
and that was the fun I had with you in your spare time.
Now and then you would drink a little too much, and I
would get angry and embarrassed for you. And you
would say "don't" when you should have said

"doesn't." When I was 15, that seemed very important.

I never told you I loved you, and I don't think you ever said those words to me. I never thought about it much, till I had a son, and I've made it a point to tell him often that I love him. He has reluctantly taken the hint, and properly prodded, he will tell me the same thing.

Truth be known, I think about you more in death than I did in life. I suspect that's because it's true that a man doesn't really grow up till his father dies. And maybe doesn't really think about what his father means to him till it's a little late. It's one of the inadequacies and maybe inequities of fatherhood.

But if it makes you feel any better, and I hope it does, for almost 25 years now, I've thought of you, asked your advice, asked your approval probably five days out of every seven. And told you how much I loved you.

Because you were a hell of a good guy.

Love,
Bill

Earl Blackwell

Earl Blackwell, known affectionately as "Mr. Celebrity," will in two years celebrate his fiftieth year as founder of *Celebrity Service*, the information and research organization whose vast espionage system (with offices in New York, Washington, Hollywood, London, Paris and Rome) keeps track of over 350,000 celebrities. He started the service in 1939 with a capital of $300.00 (borrowed from a friend) and a rented typewriter.

"Earl lives in a world of make-believe . . . where the heroes and heroines can do no wrong," Gloria Swanson once said. "He loves everybody and the feeling seems to be mutual." Ginger Rogers summed it up best when she told a reporter, "Earl keeps such close tabs on us that before I started to write my autobiography, I asked to borrow my file."

Earl is equally well known as a host, having given the most famous parties of our time both here and overseas. He was born in Atlanta, the son of Samuel and Carrie Blackwell. The following is a recreation of a letter he would like to have written to his father in 1932. The group photo is of (left to right) Earl's father Samuel, Arlene Dahl, and Fernando Lamas, at one of Earl's parties. The single photograph is of Earl himself.

Dear Dad:

I immediately thought of you yesterday when I was told the almost unbelievable news that I had been elected president of the student body. I remembered your advice the day you drove me to the university to enroll me in my freshman year. You put your hand on my shoulder and said:

"Son, you are about to start a new chapter in your young life. Some of the friends you are about to meet may last a lifetime, but just remember to always be yourself. Never pretend or try to be anything but your own natural self."

This exciting honor came to me out of the blue yesterday. I didn't run for office, never would have thought of such a thing in a million years, but without my knowledge, a fraternity brother entered my name on the ballot.

Of course, I'm thrilled, and I promise you I'll do a good job.

With much love,
Earl

Joyce Brothers

Joyce Brothers describes herself as "kind of a middle-man between the viewer and psychological literature," and her commonsense advice has won her a devoted following over the years. She became an overnight celebrity in 1955, when she appeared as a boxing expert on "The $64,000 Question" and quiz-kidded her way to $134,000 in prizes. Following her impressive quiz-show win with a doctorate in psychology, Dr. Brothers was offered a radio show in New York. Soon, the world of contemporary psychology had one of its first major superstars—a fact that aroused controversy (and a good deal of envy, one suspects) among members of Dr. Brothers' profession.

Today, Joyce Brothers' column appears in over 350 newspapers, and she is heard daily on NBC radio. Her books—including *What Every Woman Should Know about Marriage*—have become best sellers, and have been translated into 26 languages. Not bad for a boxing buff turned mother-confessor to many a troubled soul!

The daughter of Morris and Estelle Bauer, Joyce was born in New York City. On the following page is a photo of Joyce and one of her father.

Dear Daddy:

I was not at all prepared for the feeling of tremendous loss and loneliness when you died. When you experience great joy and love in a relationship, you also experience great pain. The *more* joy, the *more* pain, for our relationship was so beautiful. The morning after the funeral I looked in the mirror and knew that your death was the very worst that life could hand me and was surprised to learn how totally devastated I was and how unaccepting I was of that loss.

You were terribly angry about your illness—that you had to be the one stricken with cancer. I let you take that anger at the world out on me. I was your conduit, your release, as there was no way you could get back at the world. For the first year after your death—whenever I dreamt about you—you were still angry at me. Time has taken care of that and now you come to me in my dreams as the warm, loving man you were before you became so ill. You were a fighter, Daddy, and never could allow yourself the fact that you were dying. Oh the battle you waged!

Five years after I still think about you and how delighted you would be when something wonderful happened to me or what your advice would be when I run into a problem, whatever it may be. To this day, I cannot pass your office door without looking for you, expecting you, and not find you there working away.

In our Jewish faith, we know that the father's love cannot be replaced or substituted after death, but I have been able to fill some of that void by becoming much closer to Mother.

If the death had to occur, I am thankful you did not experience pain. I had a long time to say all the things I wanted to say to you; to tell you I loved you; to give you special treats and to have beautiful memories of our travels together. I have no regrets.

I will close now and know in my heart you have heard my thoughts.

Love,
Joyce

Dave Brubeck

When the Dave Brubeck Quartet performed at the White House in June of 1986, *The Washington Post* reported: "After an encore of 'Take the A-Train' that had even the crystal chandeliers twirling, President Reagan told Brubeck, 'I don't know how much easier you could shed 50 years in so short a time.'"

Dave Brubeck has been a household name since at least 1954, when he was the focus of a *Time* magazine cover story on the rebirth of American jazz. Perhaps you have heard his famous Quartet (with Joe Morello, Eugene Wright and Paul Desmond). Their classic album *Time Out* was an international sensation, sold well over a million copies, and became the first gold record for modern jazz.

Dave was born in Concord, California. His mother, Elizabeth, was a pianist while his dad, Howard ("Pete") Brubeck, was a cattle rancher. When Dave sent me the photo following, he said, "I am entrusting you with the ONLY photograph I have of my father and me together..." (Father, "Pete" on the left, sixteen-year-old Dave in the middle and ranch foreman, Dick Lavagnino on the right). The studio photograph is of a grown-up Dave.

Dear Dad,

When I am in some distant spot on the globe, performing before people whose lives and ways are so different from anything you or I have known, I often ask myself, "What would Dad think of me now?" I guess that's what I most want to know, even now, when I am almost the age you were when you died. What do you think of me, Dad?

And to you, I want to express my eternal gratitude for your allowing me to pursue my own career, even though it meant the end of our sharing a common way of life on the ranch. After Henry and Howard became musicians, I was your last hope for a cattleman, wasn't I? I knew it. And I honestly tried all through that first miserable pre-med year at college, when it still seemed possible that I could become a veterinarian and remain with you on the ranch. Not once did you voice your disappointment when I switched to music my second year. In fact, you seemed to understand my emotional needs better than I, because you found a way to make me feel less guilty and to keep our mutual dream alive by agreeing that if things did not work out in music, I could always come home and be partners with you. Knowing this I never felt completely defeated, even when times were most desperate. And there were a few rough seasons, when I did return

27

home with my wife and new young family for brief stays.

I remember just after my discharge from the Army (Spring of 1946) you asked me to join you driving the cattle to the mountains. I figured after being in the Army three and a half years, I was in good enough shape to keep up with "the old man," so started out with you about 3 A.M., and by noon it was obvious that I was so sore there was no way I could remain in the saddle one more minute. Knowing that you did not take kindly to any confession of tiredness or soreness, I was grateful to be bringing up the rear, while you were riding at the head of the herd. So I got off my horse and started walking, leading the horse and hoping some feeling besides pain could return to my legs and seat before you spotted me. No such luck! Just as you knew every steer, cow and calf by their idiosyncracies, you could spot anything out of the ordinary a mile away. I can still see your riding back to me. I was suddenly a child again.

"Either you get back on your horse, or put him in the truck. You can drive along behind in your truck. But don't ever let anybody see Pete Brubeck's son leading a horse!"

We both felt humiliated, angry and sad. I think that was the turning point, when it was clear to us both that our lives would really diverge.

But thank God for the truck, because we were to keep going another eight hours before we camped for the night. The cattle were so worn out they gladly settled down near the road, and we slept on the ground with only our saddle blankets for cover. You may have considered this a night's rest, but I think I got more sleep in the mudhole in Verdun.

It has been forty years since I left the cowboy and ranch life, but it has always remained a part of me. You, your friends, and the generation before you, who walked to California from the East to carve out a new life in the West, have influenced me more than you know. I admire your toughness, tenacity, honesty and humor. You taught me how to channel anger and frustration into a good life no matter what the circumstances; and your example of inner strength and self-reliance has sustained me.

I can think of no man I would rather be with right this moment. We'd share lots of laughs and good memories. Remember when you won the calf roping event at Salinas? And the time they talked you into entering the calf roping contest at the Sutter Creek Rodeo? You were 65 years old. And you said, "Give me a young man at the fence to run in and do the tying after I've roped him"—and you won!

Boy was I proud of you!

Love,
Dave

George Bush

George Bush had become a decorated hero of World War II before he was even old enough to vote. At 19, he was the youngest pilot in the U.S. Navy, and had flown numerous combat missions in the Pacific Theater. Bush's courageous disregard for personal safety won him the Distinguished Flying Cross.

By 1954—when he was only 30—Bush had become president of a highly successful offshore oil-drilling firm in Texas. In 1966, he was elected to the U.S. House of Representatives. Since then, he has served as Ambassador to the U.N., as the nation's chief diplomatic representative to China, and as Director of the C.I.A. In 1980, the Republican National Convention nominated him for Vice-President at Ronald Reagan's request.

The son of Prescott and Dorothy Bush, George was born in Milton, Massachusetts. And if you look closely at the photo on the next page—you'll see the Republican elephants on Prescott Bush's tie!

Dear Dad,

It is hard sometimes for a man to say this to another man; but I love you very much—always have, always will—

George

Leo Cherne

When Leo Cherne was presented with the Presidential Medal of Freedom, the country's highest civilian award, in 1984, the citation read in part: "Leo Cherne ... has stepped forward and with brilliance, energy, and moral passion helped this Nation overcome countless challenges."

Economist, humanitarian, sculptor, political scientist, and advisor to presidents for more than forty years, Leo Cherne helped found the Research Institute of America and is its Executive Director. The international scope and significance of Cherne's work has won him France's Legion of Honor and the Federal Republic of Germany's Commander's Cross of the Order of Merit.

Leo Cherne's sculptures include bronzes of John F. Kennedy, Lyndon B. Johnson, Abraham Lincoln and Boris Pasternak. In this, Leo has followed an artistic interest of his father, Max Cherne, who is flanked by several sculpture reproductions in the photo on the right. This snapshot shows the family store in the Bronx. The upper story of the shop served as living quarters for Max and Dora Cherne, and Leo was born there.

Dear Pop:

I have forgotten your death. But not your life. And that is quite surprising because I was, it seems to me, so little aware of it during the years we shared. The nature of your livelihood was largely responsible for that. From the moment of my birth you and Mother were totally engaged taking care of that store under the "railroad flat" which was home during my first six years. Except for the turns you took to rush upstairs for a bite (or when I was in the baby carriage in front of the store) I was alone and utterly unaware of your existence.

During the many hours when I was in the flat alone in my crib, periodically shaken by the rattle and roar of the Third Avenue Elevated line, there was no world, no people outside that room which the limits of early childhood had made my prison.

The store was called a "stationery" shop—and indeed there were writing tablets, school supplies, greeting cards. This stationery shop also had a hand operated printing press behind a drawn curtain in the back of the store, since the Gibson Christmas cards were personalized with the purchaser's name, and you provided other shopkeepers with letterheads, type set by Max Cherne, hand printed by Dora—such oddly peaceful uses for something which once you'd hoped would be a lethal instrument against tyranny.

You had been a compositor in Kishinev, printing anti-czarist diatribes, helpless cries of outrage against pogroms, until you saw the danger and futility of your efforts. And there was a chance at a life less corroding. That life was in England, where now you practiced your typesetter's "upside-down" skills legitimately. (If you could answer this letter, I would ask you how you learned to set type in so foreign a language as English, so strange compared to the familiar Hebrew and Cyrillic alphabets).

From England you moved to Canada, then to the U.S. There you met my intensely intellectual seamstress Mother, who quickly learned to become the operator of your hand press, giving life to the type you assembled in your composing "stick."

There was more in that stationery store. There were the lithographs so necessary to most homes then. And there were samples of the wooden moldings from which you made the frames. And Mother would take these pictures and the glass she cut and do the framing.

Finally, there were your two additional "articles for sale" which were to become my windows to a wider world. I never did learn what moved you to seek and be given Kodak's first distributorship for the entire Borough of the Bronx in that 138th Street location, almost as far south as one could be in the Bronx. In the store you sold Brownies and the folding cameras, you sold the rolls of film and processed the results which, especially on Monday morning, were impatiently dropped through the slot of the front door by those who had already left for work when you opened the store.

But the Eastman distributorship also obliged you to buy a car, so that you might deliver the photo supplies to the photographers scattered throughout the Bronx, most of them portrait studios so vital to those in need of tangible evidence to send to the old country with the reassurance that here was one who was safe, healthy, happy, and oh!—so prosperous. Because of that car and those deliveries, somehow, somewhere around age five, I began to join you on excursions which could hardly have been more exciting than my first trips to Cuba as an ordinary seaman, ten years later. Your Kodak "agency" provided my first "window" to the world outside.

The second window opened for me on a row of plaster portrait reproductions of famous world figures, among them, virtually every celebrated musical composer: Mozart, Wagner, Berlioz, Gounod, to name a few. In that lower class Protestant neighborhood, a proper home still "needed" a Beethoven.

And so, one of the most remarkable links between us, I am certain, was the one which involved your sculpture reproductions and mine appearing in museum shops a half-century later. I wish you had lived long enough to see my first portrait, that of Albert Schweitzer. You would have approved.

Yet, it would take me nearly sixty years and your death to realize that my "sudden" turn to sculpture, in mid-life, had its undeniable roots in that shop on 138th Street in the Bronx.

There were also the weekly two subscription tickets to the Metropolitan Opera. A seat on the fifth level, barely affordable then, was also the one characteristic luxury you looked to, year after year. Since the store required the presence of one of you to close up at ten, if a friend didn't take the second ticket, it would be my turn to join you in the magic world at 38th Street and Broadway for *The Pearl Fishers*, *Carmen*, *La Juive*, or *Lohengrin*. Even then, at six or seven, looking obliquely from a side seat in the Family Circle, I would remain awake during that endless Wagner performance lest I miss the hero's arrival on the mechanical swan.

It was purely coincidence that I was selected from those auditioned in the city's schools to become a member of the Metropolitan Opera Company's children's chorus. That stint, until my child's soprano voice left me, would provide me its 50 cents per rehearsal, one dollar per dress rehearsal, and two dollars for the rare exciting evening performance.

Dear, dear Pop, to whom, as I remember it, I spoke so little, I should have asked you why one day you put your fiddle away—never to take it out again. I didn't. A child is a child is a child.

Except for those performance evenings, the visit to Horn and Hardart's Automat on each trip to 38th Street thrilled me more than did the opera. I would not have told you that. Yet, something I cannot recall, and would like to ask you: did you ever see one of those performances with me in it, performances of *Carmen*, *La Giaconda*, *Jewels of the Madonna*, which required a children's chorus? I would so want you to tell me that you were proud.

You were so unbelievably gentle in your approach to me that it took more than 50 years for it suddenly to occur to me that you were guiding, teaching, and shaping me at least as decisively as your words might have. Not that you were awkward (compositor you!) with words. Our little flat had its share of Nietzsche, Schopenhauer, Emerson, Ingersoll, Upton Sinclair. But if you spoke of them, I have no recollection of your views.

I can only recall one harsh reprimand from you, Pop. I got along well with girls, and during high school was "hanging out" in front of a candy store surrounded by the girls as you (we had moved a block) returned from lunch at home to relieve Mother when your eyes fell on your "idler." You let out one bitter epithet—"sheik!"

There was one exception to your practice of leading by exposure instead of talk. Your passionate concern for social justice clearly made its way to me with words. And with an uncharacteristic passion of expression (more characteristic of Mother and me), you made clear that social justice to you meant the protest of maligned power imposed on those weaker.

Your store on 138th Street prospered, only to be finally destroyed in the mid-thirties by Father Coughlin's Christian Front, which made our neighborhood their stronghold. And a telephone call to me in the law office in which I practiced briefly brought me rushing from Manhattan in the subway in a vain effort to urge the "Fort Apache" Police Precinct on our corner to "do something." But at least Coughlin's mob was frightened off, leaving only shattered windows as the memento of their venom.

Similarly, though almost a decade earlier, your words, the fear and rage they radiated, brought Hitler of the Munich days alive to my consciousness. A decade later those words ignited the International Rescue Committee's vital purpose for me.

And almost thirty years later, you were already gone, when in October 1956, four days after the Hungarian Revolution began, I drove with Marcel Faust, IRC's Vienna operations chief, to Budapest to bring antibiotics, warm clothes, and some food and other medications to the student freedom fighters and to Joseph Cardinal Mindszenty two hours after his release from seven years of solitary confinement in a Soviet jail. You were beyond my telling you, as I drove eastward toward your Russia, and the Cossacks who had briefly withdrawn from Budapest, that I knew the link between my commitment to the International Rescue Committee and your risking your young life in a hiding place where you composed your anti-czarist tracts.

How I wish there were a Thornton Wilder miracle capable of bringing you back for one occasion, Pop, when President Reagan conferred the Medal of Freedom on me—and my own family was present. The distance from Kishinev to the East Room of the White House is a distance measured in different worlds, or no distance at all. How I would have liked you to hear this sentence from the citation the President read:

"His lifetime devotion to aiding his country and to serving the cause of human freedom, especially through his work on behalf of refugees, reflects the strong and generous character of a man who deserves the respect and gratitude of all Americans."

That tribute to me is actually the heart of my tribute

and debt to you. In fact, it is of you he spoke, as it is of my daughter, and with luck, will aptly describe my granddaughter as well.

On the one hand, you hardly had the time to teach me anything—yet the miracle is you left no corner of my life untouched, unaffected. Does not such power warrant at least a moment's suspension of doubt—that you were there with me in the East Room that day?

Somewhere, I think your fiddle plays again.

Love,
Leo

Norman Cousins

For people of my generation, the name of Norman Cousins will always be linked to *The Saturday Review*, a magazine that became, during his 35-year tenure as editor, one of the nation's most vigorous and influential voices in literature, politics and the arts.

Stricken with a rare collagen disease, he was given a one-in-500 chance of survival, so Cousins "laughed himself back to health," watching old Marx Brothers movies and reading humorists like Bennett Cerf.

Describing this experience resulted in his best seller, *Anatomy of an Illness*. His latest book is *The Human Adventure*, a camera story of hope for our world. "I get a kick out of challenging the odds," Cousins laughs. "It's wonderful to be able to test yourself as a guinea pig with something you believe to be true with absolute confidence, against all odds, against the authorities...."

Shown in the following photograph, Norman Cousins was born to Samuel and Sara Cousins in Union Hill, New Jersey.

Dear Pop,

I had the unusual advantage just before you died of telling you all the things a son would like to tell his father but for one reason or another did not do. What I say now, therefore, is more in the nature of emphasis than afterthought. I think of you during the Depression years, working double and triple time to keep the family going. It was during the prime of your life, yet you were blocked off from all the things that might add to the enjoyment of living. I think back on weekends and holidays that you never took. I know, in my own life, how important it is to have periods of restoration and enjoyment. Indeed, this kind of balance is necessary for survival. I suppose none of us at the time fully appreciated what you did, but I certainly do now.

Love,
Norman

Bob Cummings

A lot of us who know Bob Cummings only as the star of his own long-running television series don't realize that as a youngster his chief interest was aeronautical engineering. Orville Wright, a patient and friend of Cummings' physician father, was Bob's godfather and a later influence in his love of aviation. When he was 27, Cummings received the first flight instructor rating ever issued.

By that time, however, Bob had turned to acting. Awarded a scholarship to the Academy of Dramatic Arts in New York, he worked in England and returned to Broadway under the name of "Blade Conway," "England's youngest actor, producer and director." As "Conway," Bob (oops! I mean "Blade"!) starred with Fanny Brice in "The Ziegfield Follies."

As the British craze ended, he went to Hollywood and changed back to Bob Cummings, typical American. Starring roles in movies followed—and you may remember him in such greats as *King's Row* and Hitchcock's *Dial M for Murder.* On television, his role in "Twelve Angry Men" won him an Emmy.

The son of Charles and Ruth Cummings, Bob was

born in Joplin, Missouri. He and his dad are pictured in the snapshot. He wrote me that this was the last picture of his father before his death.

Dear Dad:

I sadly realized the other day that I never told you how proud I am of you and all your accomplishments, not only as a physician and surgeon and a highly principled man, but also in the field of music with your excellent singing voice. Your subtle (and sometimes not so subtle) guidance, along with Mother's patient and steadfast teaching, have given me the answers at every turn and twist of my journey. When I've felt as if I've come to a dead end, into my mind pops one or more of your oft repeated philosophies, such as "You can accomplish anything in the Universe by persistently *acting* with *all your heart* as if it's already accomplished!"

Mother has told me many times how you carried me in your arms out into the dark night behind our home in Joplin the year I was born and did your best to show me the wonders of Halley's Comet. Of course that was in 1910, I never told you, but I don't remember it. Here we are in 1985 and Halley's is back again. I'm now in California and because I can legitimately claim that my daddy, Dr. Charles Clarence Cummings, showed me Edmund Halley's Comet during the last visit in 1910, I'm going to be invited to Griffith's Observatory here in Los Angeles to view the

Comet through the huge telescope there. The reason because I'm automatically a member of "The Two Timers Club," those who have viewed the ball of fire with the long tail twice.

A million thanks Dad and Mommy for your amazing foresight. Maybe I'll be able, someday, to tell you in person how it looked the second time around.

> Your ever grateful and loving
> 75 year old son,
>
> Charles Clarence Robert Orville Cummings
> Star of Stage, Screen, Radio,
> Television and Geritol

Jacques D'Amboise

I think all of us who watched ABC-TV's "20/20" on Christmas Day in 1986, and saw the segment on Jacques d'Amboise, agreed with ABC's Bob Brown when he said: "This is a story about how thousands of children year after year earn the right to jump into the spotlight for at least a few seconds, because a man who was once one of the greatest stars of ballet has made it his business to teach them how. In doing so, he has sometimes transformed them."

Founder and artistic director of the National Institute of Dance in New York, as well as one of the finest classical dancers of our time, d'Amboise's goal is to provide the opportunity for children, especially boys, to discover the arts, using dance as a catalyst.

In addition to his long association with the New York City Ballet, Jacques has also appeared in hit films like *Seven Brides for Seven Brothers* and *The Best Things in Life are Free*. Presently he is working on preparations for an hour-long ballet involving moveable sculpture that will premiere in 1987 as NDI/New York's Event of the Year.

Born in Dedham, Massachusetts, Jacques is the son of Andrew and Georgette d'Amboise. He regrets he has no available photograph of his father.

51

Dear Papa—

Your wonderful stories, your taste and knowledge of music—the joy and command of language and love of words—all these I remember you gave to your children as well as the labors of a lifetime for us.

But most precious are those many, many nights when you stroked my hair and forehead while murmuring "cachette—cachette" to help send me to sleep.

All of it and you, I hold close to my heart.

Love you,
Jacques

Phyllis Diller

Phyllis Diller wrote me that when her dad, Perry Driver, died at the age of 86 in 1945, the letter that follows was found folded and dog-eared in his wallet —a clue, perhaps, that a child's words of love and gratitude can mean worlds to a parent at *any* age. Perry Driver did not live long enough to see Phyllis, a "late bloomer" by her own admission, become the world's leading female stand-up comic. But he probably wouldn't have been surprised that his pixie-sized daughter decided, once her own children were grown, to prepare a night club act and hit the road. Her first time out, Phyllis was booked at San Francisco's "Purple Onion"—for two weeks. She stayed for 89!

From that point on, Ms. Diller's career skyrocketed. She has starred in three television series, countless specials, and has been a guest star on hundreds of top-rated shows. "I love TV," she says. "It's not my fault if the tubes blow out when I laugh."

The real Phyllis Diller is quite down to earth and seriously caring about everyone she meets. She and her stage persona share a rare good humor, a warmth and love of people—qualities for which she thanks her father, Perry Driver, in the letter that follows.

P. M. DRIVER

LIMA, OHIO,

Candidate for

Representative for Allen County

Subject to Democratic Primary, to
be held May 17th, 1910

Dear Dad,

Thank you for all the important things you have given me, a fine education, good genes and a wonderful secure childhood. You have passed along to me all the best including a sense of humor. I want you to know how much I appreciate what you have given me.

Love,
Phyllis

Eileen Ford

Eileen Ford's career is truly the stuff of legend—in fact her story could easily earn her the title of the female Horatio Alger. While attending Barnard College, she took summer jobs as a model. Following graduation, she met and married Jerry Ford, with whom she launched the famous Ford Model Agency.

The idea for the agency came almost accidentally in 1946. Eileen, awaiting the birth of her first child, would take phone calls for a couple of her model friends. Soon, there were a dozen models and a small walk-up office on Second Avenue. Within a short time, the Ford Agency had become the premier model agency in the world, its girls gracing the covers of major magazines. Many went on to spectacular careers on stage and film: Jane Fonda, Suzy Parker, Candice Bergen, Ali McGraw, Lauren Hutton, Brooke Shields —the list goes on and on.

The Fords have gone from a two-room, one-coffee-pot office to their own red-brick building on Manhattan's East Side. Three of their four grown children also work at the agency, making the business truly a family affair. Perhaps it's this strong sense of family, which Eileen got particularly from her dad, Nathaniel Otto (photo, page 58), that makes the Ford Agency unique in the world of beauty and fashion. The other photo is of Eileen.

58

Dear Dad:

I have been asked to write a letter to you somewhere up in that great Fathers' Place in the sky.

If ever I were to tell you something I have never said, it would be because it is just dawning on me how much I owe you for instilling in me and my brothers a great sense of honesty and responsibility in dealing with others; and, in some way, you got the message through to our four children.

When we meet again, I will thank you in person; but truthfully, I hope that the meeting will not be for a very long time.

Your loving daughter,
Eileen

Uta Hagen

Few acting careers can match Uta Hagen's for sheer range and versatility. She is as comfortable—and as convincing—playing Desdemona in Shakespeare's *Othello* as she is playing Blanche DuBois in Tennessee Williams' *A Streetcar Named Desire*. You may have seen her in one of these roles—or as the tough, foul-mouthed Martha in Edward Albee's *Who's Afraid of Virginia Woolf?*, a role that won Ms. Hagen awards on both sides of the Atlantic. Her book *Respect for Acting* is now in its seventeenth printing, while thousands of readers have enjoyed her *Love for Cooking* and her personal memoir *Sources*.

The daughter of Oskar and Thyra Hagen, Uta was born in Göttigen, Germany. The letter that follows was written to her father while she was on a much needed vacation, after a two year engagement as Blanche DuBois in *Streetcar*. She asked me to print the letter unedited, explaining that "the letter was obviously written in a surge of emotion and should stay as it is." I am happy to comply with Ms. Hagen's wishes, for the letter, as well as the photo with her father on the next page, have a warmth and intimacy that reveal much about her feelings for her dad.

Vernet-les-Bains, June 17, 1950

Papa, my darling:

If my pencil could only follow the rush of my feelings and what I have to tell you, and if I could be patient enough to write everything to you as it has happened in the past few days, I imagine it would fill several volumes. But the main thing is that I suddenly realized so fully that what I am, you and Mama have made me and that I owe you so much more than life— my whole perception and everything that makes life full and rich you have given me. What I see and smell and feel and my capability of receiving things fully comes from you and that you opened all my senses to these things so very early! When I walk into a cathedral and feel a vague mysteriousness of past ages first because of a musty, wood-stove incense smell, it comes as such a *memory* (not even new experience) of what you showed me, or how you stimulated emotions toward it as a child—before I could rationalize it or make it a conscious, organic part of me, which I'm just beginning to do now. Even down to a sense of language and communication which you gave me so long, long ago.

My whole leave-taking was so abrupt and weird and

suddenly I was in Paris at the Hotel Voltaire (19 Quai Voltaire) where I'll be again by June 26th (when you get a chance to write), looking out over the Seine, across at the Louvre; riding through the Tuileries in an open carriage; drinking Pernod at the Café du Dome, or lunch at, or cocktails in Noel Coward's Maxims on the Place Vendôme or Pierre Blanchard at the Theatre Louis Jouvet, etc., etc.,—all in one and a half *days*. And then a long journey to Toulouse and all its Cathedrals—so weird a mixture of Roman and Byzantine; and a long car trip through Southern France and Carcassonne and along the Côte d'Azure with Perpignan, Prades, and way off into the Pyrennees Orientals to Vernet-les-Bains, where I am now (another 2 *days*); and my head aches and swims with impressions and pains of emotion.

Last night and this morning were almost too much. The concerts are in the Cathedral. Thousands of people, sitting, standing, leaning in such an atmosphere of hushed reverence that even before a note of music starts your heart hurts you! And then, when Casals comes out in front of the altar and orchestra, these same thousands rise to their feet, with no sound except the upward movement of their bodies until Casals nods and sits and they sit again and for an hour or more these bodies don't breathe except to the music and I cry and cry. Of course it is all Bach and the Angels sing and sweep and soar and weep through the arches of the cathedral and you almost don't want to breathe anymore. The concentration and purity of intention of all the musicians makes it almost impossible to look at them, so you shut your eyes.

And at the end the thousands of people leave in the same silence and only in more awe than with which they came. The old men with beards, the old women with shawls and the very young children make up the greater part of the audience, but the American, English and Parisians feel the same simple greatness as do the peasants. It's more than unforgettable. I don't know words for it.

At nine this morning we were at a rehearsal that was terrifying in its concentration. Led by Casals who controls everything by his quiet mildness. He said he was "so grateful to the musicians for having come from all over the world to play with him, brought here by Alexander Schneider—who took pity on my silence!" When I get back I feel I should take a trip to Madison to tell you all in person. Four more days here with all concerts and rehearsals. Then Rapallo for three days before I get back to Paris. I love you and thank you with my whole soul.

Your Uti

Monty Hall

Between 1964 and 1977, Monty Hall, as co-owner, star and packager of the T.V. game show, "Let's Make a Deal," gave away over 30 million dollars to costumed adults from all over the United States. In 1984, he was back, hosting a new version, which is currently in syndication throughout the country, along with his very latest show, "Split Second." In addition to his work as a game show host, Hall has frequently been a guest on talk show programs across the country.

Monty Hall's life away from the television cameras has been as important as that on stage. He has travelled the United States, Canada and Europe, speaking and performing on behalf of countless charities. Hall is as proud of this work as he is of his TV career. He was read into the Congressional Record for organizing the all-star show for families of the victims of the tragic Wichita State and Marshall University air disasters. And in 1983, he received the prestigious Variety Club's International Humanitarian Award.

The son of Maurice and Rose Halparin, Monty Hall was born in Winnipeg, Manitoba. The priceless photo on the next page reveals the happiness and love between father and son. The snapshot shows Monty, at twelve months of age, with his dad.

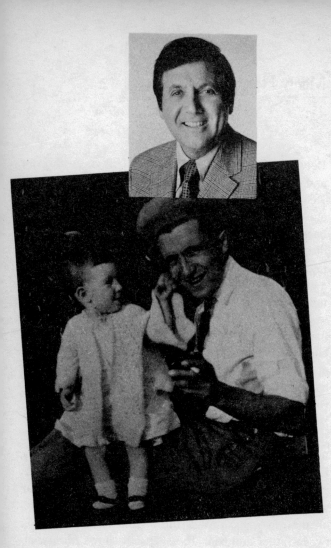

Dear Dad,

It's three years since you've left us, and with the sale of your condo which was just completed this week, a final curtain has rung down. I remember how you looked forward to our visits to Palm Springs. You asked for our estimated arrival time and when we drove up, you were always on the front lawn eagerly awaiting us.

In the earlier days, it was both you and Mother; then after her death, you alone—a little more eager, more nervous, as if time were running out and you had so little to spare that each moment we ran behind schedule cheated you of your delicious pleasure with your family. I know what the visits meant to you, and they were always the same. Questions about my career, my income, my future. Teasing the grandchildren was your favorite sport, but they in return badgered you to give up smoking.

And then all too soon, the weekend was over, the car loaded up and pulled away. You stood in the driveway, smiling and waving—but we knew you had a catch in your throat. You kept asking yourself,

"Will there be a next time?" And then—one day, there wasn't. And we all are cheated by time.

Monty

Roger Horchow

If you find an elephant in your mailbox, don't blame last night's party, blame Roger Horchow. The innovative creator of the "Horchow Collection," an upscale mail-order business based in Dallas, prides himself on finding the rare and the beautiful—and bringing it to your front door with a minimum of hassle.

Born in Cincinnati to Reuben and Beatrice Horchow, Roger was educated at Yale and continues to have a close association with his *alma mater*. A Woodrow Wilson Fellow, he is very active in a variety of civic, educational and cultural projects across the country. He serves on the Board of Directors of the American Institute of Public Service, the National Trust for Historic Preservation, and the Asthma and Allergy Foundation; he serves, too, as vice-chairman of the American Heart Association. There is time, too, for writing in Roger Horchow's busy life. He is the author of *Elephants in Your Mailbox* (1980—and I'm not kidding about the title!), as well as *Living with Style* (1981).

Roger Horchow's dad appears in the photograph on the next page, and if you look closely, you'll see Roger himself in a frame on the shelf!

Dear Dad,

It all turned out very well, just as you always said it would. I didn't always believe that all I had to do was my very best and it would "work out."

You taught me to make and be responsible for my own decisions. You made me consider all the alternatives and you helped me develop my lifelong exercise of considering what's the worst that could happen before making a commitment or making a big decision.

I was able to pursue my mail-order idea and start my own business because you taught me how to analyze the situation and make a decision. Better still, you allowed me my education and my freedom from you.

As an army officer and a college professor I know you made many sacrifices for me. I love you for being the best father you could be, and I'll try with my three daughters to do as well, or better!

Much love,
Roger

Pat Howell

Pat and his wife Joan have recently returned to live in the house in which he grew up. "Coming back here to live," Pat says, "is like running into yourself as a child, and having that child's emotions fully reawakened."

Pat Howell's "homecoming" has happened after decades spent in work that has taken him all over the world. Born in Dallas to Texas pioneers Roy and Fay Howell, Pat became a United Press staff correspondent after World War II. In the years following, he served as a consultant to political, economic and relief projects in Third World developing countries. Drawn increasingly to the search for more basic answers to the problems of developing peoples in an ever more rapidly changing world, Pat went back to school late in his life and received a doctorate in psychology. He continues his interest in human development as chairman of the board of the Western Human Science Fund.

Both author and publisher, Pat and his wife Joan, a former top model, have written *Embodied Mind*, and Pat is now head of house of Saybrook Publishing Company. The photo on the right shows Pat's dad walking in the neighborhood where he was a familiar figure for most of his 96 years.

Dear Dad,

I'm writing to tell you what I didn't say on my visit.
I came angry and exasperated; the shrubbery was an
overgrown tangle. The house where I was born and
grew up was a derelict. Aunt Helen had written hinting
I was an unnatural child to let you live like that. Also
that it was a disgrace to the neighborhood. More, that
your behavior was a disgrace to the neighborhood.

I was thinking of my last visit staying at the house
when you woke me up at 4 A.M. to go over to the River
Café. I said it was night and got back into bed. You
got belligerent and said, "I've been going to the River
Café at 4 o'clock every day for the last 60 years. I'm
not about to stop going because you're here." I pulled
the covers over my head and said, "Go on. Find out
for yourself."

The police brought you back around 5:00 for
loitering around the closed café in the middle of the
night. They also gave me some dirty looks for letting a
95-year-old man wander around in the middle of the
night. I had to agree with them.

And then you would walk through the park down
to the lake wearing your house slippers with rubber
bands around your insteps to keep them on—and in
the winter too. Why you didn't get frostbite I will
never know.

Everyone agreed that you had to go to a nice retirement home and that it was up to me to see that you did.

You must have known what I was going to say. Remember? We were sitting down in the dining room in our old places. There was food crusted on your coat. Ever since mother died it had been getting worse. You were rubbing the arm of the old chair. I took a deep breath to begin my ultimatum.

You pushed yourself up and moved over to the window. As you put your hand on the old faded drapes a halo of dust puffed out. You said, "she's here—everywhere—I can't leave her."

You remember? You looked at me, really looked at me and got back in your chair. What could I say? There was nothing left of all that I had meant to say. The low light was slanting across the room; we sat there silent, two old men.

I said, "I love you." And you said, "I love you." You had never said that to me. I hadn't ever said that before to you.

I'm writing to say that I'm glad you lived long enough for it to happen.

Lucy is going to keep coming twice a week. She's going to go on trying to keep your clothes clean (you won't let her). She's going to keep trying to take the drapes to be cleaned, etc., and you won't let her. Arthur is going to keep trying to trim the shrubbery every month, and you won't let him.

And some winter morning at 4 o'clock, while I'm warm in bed, you'll get up and dress. You'll be wearing your carpet slippers and you'll wander off to the park or to the River Café when they're not open. You'll slip on the ice and not be able to get up, and you'll freeze to death there alone in the dark. Some stranger will find you.

So I'm grieving and worrying—but that's OK. I know you are keeping faith with the woman you love and the life you have lived.

God Bless You,
Pat

Kathy Keeton

From child prodigy with London's Royal Ballet to one of the highest paid women executives in the world today: such has been the astonishing career of Kathy Keeton, president of *Omni* magazine. The daughter of South African farmers, Keith and Queenie Keeton, Kathy was stricken by polio as a small child. Her study of ballet in London (still a passionate interest) was inspired by her efforts to overcome the physical limitations of her childhood polio.

In London Kathy met Bob Guccione. "When he saw my collection of business papers, my charts, and commodities analysis, we started a business discussion that continues even today. Bob ended up offering me a fulltime job with his new *Penthouse* magazine as an advertising sales representative." The rest is publishing history. As Vice Chairman of Penthouse International Ltd., Kathy works closely with Publisher Bob Guccione on every phase of corporate development; and as president of *Omni* Publications, she is instrumental in the planning, day-to-day strategy, and direction of the world's leading consumer-science magazine, *Omni*. She has also been selected "Outstanding Woman in Publishing" by the March of Dimes.

Kathy Keeton and her dad Keith are pictured together on the next page.

Dear Dad,
   I Love You . . . you are the very best Dad a girl could ever have.

                              With all my love,
                              Kathy

Art Linkletter

A television and radio star for more than 45 years, Art Linkletter has performed in two of the longest running shows in broadcasting history: "House Party," on day time CBS-TV and radio (for 25 years), and "People Are Funny," on night time NBC-TV and radio (for 19 years). These shows—which made Linkletter a regular guest in virtually every American home—topped the rating charts for years and earned several Emmy nominations. In addition, Art has starred in numerous television specials, including such memorable ones as "Inside Beverly Hills," "Christmas in the Holy Land," and "Come Love the Children."

Art has been writing books since 1950, and his list now numbers 16. Best known and loved is his *Kids Say the Darndest Things*, one of the 15 best sellers in American publishing history and #1 for two straight years on the non-fiction charts.

In 1962 Linkletter was named Grandfather of the Year, an honor he still prizes the most highly among the many he has received over the years. An orphan from Moosejaw, Saskatchewan, Art was later adopted by the Baptist missionary, Rev. Fulton Linkletter, and his wife. No photo of Art's dad was available for inclusion in this book.

Dear Dad:

You finally got your wish.

I know that you were unhappy when I went into broadcasting and even unhappier when some of my early clients were cigarette and wine sponsors because as a devoted Baptist minister you wanted me to be a preacher and you certainly did not want me to be persuading people to smoke or drink wine.

But in the years that have passed, my commercial career in broadcasting has led me on a roundabout way over 45 years to a lecturing career which now takes me to hundreds of audiences all over the nation talking about drug abuse prevention and the role of the family and the church in rehabilitation. So you see, Dad, in a way I have become a preacher, after all, and you will be especially happy to learn that I appear in churches such as Rev. Schuller's Crystal Cathedral over national networks, Jim Bakker's PTL and Pat Robertson's 700 Club (CBN network), as well as many individual churches. As a natural born missionary, you will be gratified and even astounded to learn of my work with World Vision, traveling to Africa, India, and Vietnam to help feed & clothe hurting people and bringing them a message from the Good Book. When I used to play the triangle on street corners in the small band that preceded your evangelical efforts, I never knew I was being prepared for a life in the public eye, and your work with "jailbirds" and ex-convicts in a mission in San Diego was a forerunner for my appearances now with Chaplain Ray at huge penitentiaries such as San Quentin and Attica.

In brief, Dad, you can feel that all those years at your knee hearing you read the Bible as a child did have the eventual outcome that you prayed for.

Rest in peace,
Your son,
Art

Loretta Lynn

When *Ladies Home Journal* named Loretta Lynn among its 100 most important women in America, the honor was understandable. Far beyond her reputation as a performer, she has developed into that rarest of social creatures: a woman who can be admired by career women and homemakers alike. In 1985 Loretta received the American Music Awards "Award of Merit" in recognition of her exemplary career.

Loretta recently ran into Rod Stewart (whose music she loves) at a New York hotel. Just as she was about to walk up and say hello to him, a camera-waving fan rushed up. "No pictures, please," Stewart asked. To which the fan replied. "I don't want a picture of you—I want one of Loretta." "I could've crawled under a log," says Loretta in wonderment, "but Rod was a real good sport about it all."

Even if you're not a country music fan, I'm sure you saw *Coal Miner's Daughter*, the movie version of Loretta's life. Born in Butcher Hollow, Kentucky to Ted and Clara Webb, Loretta says "Daddy was real gentle with kids. That's why I expected so much out of marriage, figuring that all men should be steady and pleasant, like my Daddy." Take a look at the photo of father and daughter.

Dear Daddy,

You know, we've always been a close family but we never said much about it. I wish I had told you how much I love you. I just took it for granted that you knew. But ever since you've been gone, I make it a point to tell all of the family how much I love them anytime we're together and have to part again.

I also wish you could have lived to see me sing. You always believed in me, and I guess you were right.

I miss you more than ever, Daddy.

Loretta

Ed McMahon

"My philosophy is simple," says Ed McMahon, "I like what I do, I like being busy and I love being a good second banana." Ed likes it so much, in fact, that this year he will celebrate his 25th anniversary on "The Tonight Show," starring Johnny Carson. And if being Carson's sidekick weren't enough, who hasn't fantasized (c'mon, be honest!) about Ed's announcing *their* name in one of those multimillion-dollar publishers' giveaways?

You've probably seen his own "Star Search" show, an effort to seek out and support young talent, as well as his "TV Bloopers" series. In addition, Ed has been featured in films such as *Slaughter's Big Rip Off, The Incident*, and *Fun With Dick and Jane*. He has appeared too on Broadway in comedy, *The Impossible Years*. He and his wife Victoria, who adopted a baby girl—Katherine Mary—in December of 1985, have also received the Susie Award of the Eddie Cantor Charitable Foundation for their many humanitarian efforts.

Born to Edward and Eleanor McMahon, Ed was raised in Lowell, Massachusetts, where he also got started in his radio career. A fire at Ed's home destroyed many precious family mementos, including all the photos he once had of his father.

Dear Dad,

The greatest thing happened to me today. After taping "Who Do You Trust" with Johnny Carson, we walked next door to Sardi's to get a drink and during the course of our libation Johnny said, "When we start the show in September . . ." I did a double-take and after a long pause said, "What do you mean 'we'?" Johnny replied, "Are you kidding, you know I'm taking you with me." What he was talking about was the "The Tonight Show."

That was 23 years ago, Dad, and we are still going strong. So if you were ever worried about me finding a steady job . . . I did!

Your loving son,
Edward

Robert Merrill

Acclaimed by critics as "one of the great natural baritones of the century," Robert Merrill has a devotion to baseball that is almost as legendary as his love of singing. Indeed, he once pitched for a semi-pro team in order to help pay for singing lessons. His recording of the National Anthem is played at the home games of the New York Yankees, and it has become a tradition for him to sing the anthem live at Yankee opening games. This "Star Spangled Baritone" even has his pinstripes with Number 1½ on the back!

However, it is the Metropolitan Opera stage that has been Robert Merrill's choice "stadium" for more than forty years. It was not always so. When his career began, he played the Borscht Belt, working with Danny Kaye, Red Skelton, and other great comedians. For a time he had a night club act with Louis Armstrong. But when Toscanini first heard the young baritone in 1946, Merrill's break came. He became one of Toscanini's favorites and collaborated with him several times over the ensuing years.

The son of Abraham and Lillian Miller, Robert Merrill was born in Brooklyn. Though no photo of his dad was available, I know his father would have beamed proudly when his son won the "Father of the Year Award in Music" in 1983. The photo on the next page is of Robert Merrill.

Dear Dad:

You have been in my thoughts so very often since the day you left us.

We're nearing the end of the baseball season now and I remember so clearly the time you took me and a few friends of mine to the Yankee Stadium to see the great New York Yankees. I was only eight at the time and never forgot the subway ride and the anticipation of entering the Stadium. There we were at last in the bleachers and lo and behold my hero, Babe Ruth, hit a home run right smack into our section. My excitement instantly turned to disappointment when one of my friends caught the Babe's ball. How I wanted that ball! I asked you to get it for me Pop, and of course you said "No, no he caught it and it belongs to him now."

And as fate would have it, my friend's father came over that same night to thank you for taking us all to the game, and gently placed that magical ball in my hand. So you see Pop, if not for you I might never have become a Yankee fan!

How many times I wish you were alive to see me standing in the pitcher's box (looking up at that section of the bleachers where we stood when I was just a little guy) singing the National Anthem for so many

World Series and playoffs. And finally, I wish you were here to enjoy it with me.

God bless, I will always be indebted to you.

Much, much love,
Bob

PS: Say, maybe you are listening to me sing the National Anthem! Do you think you could get the Babe to listen too?

Peter Nero

While I was in the process of editing this book, Julius Nierow, Peter Nero's dad, sent me a small collection of photos. "Please take care of them," Julius wrote me, "they are our priceless possession." In each photo, Peter is identified by his father as "my music man." No description could be more apt. Peter Nero's musical career has taken him to recording studios (30 albums, two Grammys), and, more recently, to the nation's concert halls. Since its establishment in 1979, Nero has been music director and maestro of the Philly Pops Orchestra—and he performs about 100 concerts each year with his trio, as well as other symphony orchestras.

Peter Nero is one of those rare musicians who seems equally at home in the world of classical, jazz, film and pop music. His 1962 album, *The Colorful Peter Nero*, was a sensational hit, and won him a Grammy. The following year, he was nominated for a Golden Globe for his score and title song for the Jane Fonda comedy, *Sunday in New York*.

The son of Julius and Mary Nierow, Peter was born in New York City. The letter that follows—directly after the photos of Peter and of a young Peter with his dad—was written in 1977 on the occasion of Julius' "retirement."

June 8, 1977

Dear Dad,

It is with deep regret that I cannot be with you to celebrate your retirement. However, I wanted to let you know that my thoughts, good wishes and love are with you always and especially on this occasion.

I think "retirement" is not an accurate word to describe the impending change in your life. I *know* you will remain more active than ever no matter what you choose to do. "Retirement" really signifies the birth of a new phase of your life—one in which I hope you will desire to please yourself. Until now, you have derived great pleasure from doing for others, and I have nothing but love, admiration and respect for that. God knows, you have paid your dues and I wish you all the happiness in the world with your new life.

Just as Portnoy, via Phillip Roth and Freudian psychiatry, maligned the Jewish mother, the Jewish father has run a close second as another victim of the human adult's attempt to rationalize his own shortcomings. At this point in my life, I prefer to define "adult" as one who accepts his shortcomings as his own and attributes his successes to his parents. Quite a switch. The older I get, the more clearly I can look back and put my early environment in its proper perspective.

You always sacrificed your own desires for the good of those around you, and your children were no exception. Even though you couldn't tell a "C" sharp from the Nierow flat, you nevertheless were sensitive enough to recognize my needs and love for music. I'll never forget those 3 X 5 cards that contained the rewrites of all the notes you took while you attended my piano lessons. When I reached eleven years of age, you went into hock to buy me a real Steinway piano. For those things, I thank you.

You "encouraged" me, against my wishes, to travel 31 stops daily, in both directions, on the IRT Subway to attend the High School of Music and Art and they turned out to be some of the best years of my life (not the subway—the school). For that, I thank you.

When I was treated unfairly in school (a 50 and 4 "N's" in Spanish) *you* travelled the 31 stops and fought for me. Justice was done, and for that, I thank you.

When I was 19, and winning TV talent shows, you not only protested in writing to the one that I lost ("Chance of a Lifetime") you also had to be restrained from punching the host in the nose. You had seen that the show was rigged and your written protests paid off, since two weeks later the host was forced to make an on-the-air speech about the "legitimacy" of the show's methods of selecting a winner. (The pots-and-pans-salesmen-turned-comedians who won soon returned to selling pots and pans.)

I could and would like to go on forever reminiscing about similar incidents and recounting all the other things you did for me, both big and small, but I think the most important thing you did for me was to be the kind of person you were. Children *do* imitate their parents and if I could only be half the man you are, I would consider myself very lucky, indeed.

You were strong; you were my rock and for a child to grow up without a "rock" is like Washington trying to cross the Delaware without a boat. No task was ever too challenging for you; by this, you taught me that courage is not trying to conquer people, but oneself; that success in anything can only be achieved by determination and plain old hard work. You used to say: "There's only one way to do it and that's the right way." I used to laugh and say, "You mean, there's only one way to do it and that's *your* way"—typical teenage "schtick." It took me 30 years to realize that your way *was* the right way and for that, I thank you.

You were also the fairest person I ever knew. I always felt I could bring a problem to you and get a solution that was free from personal prejudice—you suddenly clarified very complex teen problems, always with an eye toward reality. You did the greatest impression of King Solomon I have ever seen or heard.

No matter how busy you were, trying to provide the best for your family, you always somehow made time for them, too. I knew no other father who worked as many hours as you, who slept as little as you, and who still managed to call home 10 times a day. I'm afraid that in my teen years I mistook your hard work and dedication to your job as rejection of your family. I think I was probably a little jealous of your other 130 children (your job at the orphanage)— a case of sibling rivalry measuring 8.5 on the Richter Scale. But, now that I know what it's like for a man to bear the responsibility of a family and try to provide for its security and future, I can understand your plight. It must not have been easy to put in a 20 hour day and get rebuked for it—all understandable, but nevertheless difficult to cope with at the time.

And so, my father, rest easy, because time not only heals but also educates, and all those speeches about "you'll thank me later," while they were met with cries of disbelief and antagonism at the time, paid off, because I *do* thank you, and *later* it surely is—but not *too* late, I hope.

Love,
Your Son,
Peter

Minnie Pearl

"She's apple pie and clothes dried in the sun and the smell of fresh bread baking . . . and she's forgotten to take the $1.98 price tag off her hat." That's how Sarah Ophelia Colley Cannon describes her characterization of Minnie Pearl, who has entertained millions since she first appeared on the stage of Nashville's Grand Old Opry in 1940.

Minnie Pearl is distinctly a stage personality, but there is some of her in Sarah Ophelia Cannon, who developed the character a little bit by accident. During the Depression, Sarah had a job travelling from small town to small town in the South, putting on amateur musical comedies for church and civic groups. Those events coupled with the songs and stories she heard from rural people helped create Minnie Pearl—the only comedy star ever admitted to the Country Music Hall of Fame.

Sarah Cannon happily admits that her role as Minnie Pearl with the Grand Ole Opry opened up a new life. "I was young," she says, "I would flirt with the audience, really ham it up to get extra encores." She remains, to this day, grateful for her daddy's influence and love. As she always says on the Opry, "I'm just so *proud* to be here." The daughter of Thomas and Fannie Colley, Sarah Cannon was born in Centerville, Tennessee. Her photo and her dad's photo are on the following page.

Dear Daddy,

You never knew how much I loved you. I told you, I'm sure, but never in the right way—nor enough.

Thank you for so many things. For making me aware of beauty in nature; for teaching me bird calls when I was a tot; for teaching me to love to read; for teaching me to respect the dignity of others, regardless of creed, race or color; for sharing your wonderful sense of humor; for teaching me to be proud of my country "raisin';" and for teaching me to tell the truth (the *hard* way, by catching me in a lie!).

Most of all though, Daddy, you taught me to love God and the Golden Rule. You lived by that and taught all of your children by example rather than words.

I still miss you, Daddy. I could go on and on. I still love you devotedly.

> Sarah Ophelia Colley Cannon
> (Minnie Pearl)

Gary Player

One of the greatest golfing legends of all times, Gary Player began his professional career at the age of 17 and continues his dominance in the world of golf with his emergence on the Senior Tour. During his professional career he has compiled a world record that no one has come close to equaling, winning 125 tournaments in 11 different countries. These have included 9 major championships (The British Open, 3 times; the U.S. Open, one time; the PGA Championship, 2 times; the Masters, 3 times). Small wonder that Player has come to be known as the "International Ambassador of Golf." He is one of only four men in the history of the sport who has won the Grand Slam of Golf and is a winner of the coveted Bobby Jones award.

He is married to Vivienne Verway, an excellent golfer in her own right, holding a 2 handicap when she was playing regularly. The Players have six children and one granddaughter, who was born in 1985. Gary's son Wayne became a professional golfer in 1982 after a brief but distinguished amateur career.

The son of Francis and Muriel Player, Gary was born in Johannesburg, South Africa. The letter that follows is one Gary would like to have written to his dad (photo, right), who was in South Africa at the time.

Dear Dad:

I feel very sad leaving for the USA today, as I know you are not feeling well. Thank goodness for golf though, because it enabled you to travel with me and see a lot of the world and to bring us even closer together.

I want you to know how much I appreciate your sitting and watching me practice for hour upon hour. The love you have given me as a father, I can assure you it will never ever be forgotten. Often I feel low when I think that Mommy never saw me win one of the world titles, but I guess she really did see it all from above.

You know, Dad, I'm so grateful we were so poor and that we all had to struggle, because when I'm faced with adversity on the course, I face up to it like a man. You have never been shy to cry, and you have the best laugh of any human on this earth. All your grandchildren say to me, "I love Grandpa because he always makes me laugh."

I will phone you and let you know how things are going in the USA. I will never forget how proud you were that the USA landed on the moon first yesterday. I will tell all Americans how you ran into my room and said, "*We* landed on the moon; *we* beat the Russians."

If ever you die whilst I'm away, I will fly back immediately as a matter of great love and respect for you even though you say I must not.

Dad, I love you very much and keep busy as you can.

Your loving son,
Gary

Pete Rozelle

Pete Rozelle went directly from college to the broadcasters' booths and practice facilities of the L.A. Rams, where he was publicity director and, later (1957-1960), general manager. In January, 1960, Rozelle was elected the sixth Commissioner of the NFL. He became Commissioner of all major professional football with the merger agreement between the NFL and the American Football League in June, 1966.

Pete and his wife Carrie and their family live in a suburb of New York City. The Rozelles are active in numerous public service organizations, including the United Way of America. In 1983, Pete and Carrie were recipients of United Way's distinguished Alexis de Tocqueville Society Award which "recognizes persons who have rendered outstanding service as volunteers in their own community or nationally." Mr. Rozelle also received the 1985 Robie Humanitarian Award, which is granted annually by the Jackie Robinson Foundation.

A native Californian, Pete was born to Raymond and Hazel Rozelle. Pete's grateful admiration for his dad, of whom no photo was available, is warmly evident in the letter that follows. The photo is of Pete himself.

Dear Dad:

Thank you with all my heart for giving me that second-hand Royal typewriter when I was 12 years old and for taking me to the many sporting events that you did.

You were responsible for channeling me into sports publicity as a vocation which led to later administrative jobs in the sports world.

Love,
Pete

P.S. I am still amazed at the fact that your family circumstances did not permit you to go to college and yet you could 'wipe out' a Sunday newspaper crossword puzzle (in ink yet).

Wally Schirra

Remember those first exhilarating years of the U.S. space program? A youthful John Kennedy told us we'd be walking on the moon by the end of the decade (the 1960s)—and we *were*! One of the men who made that achievement possible was Wally Schirra. Among the first Americans chosen for astronaut training in 1959. Capt. Schirra, U.S.N., went on to log 295 hours and 14 minutes in space, becoming the only astronaut to have flown Mercury, Gemini and Apollo missions. As Command Pilot on Apollo VII in 1968, Schirra executed maneuvers essential to the success of America's first lunar landing in 1969. That mission also gave us another "first": millions of us watched, with a mixture of awe and incredulity, while the activities of Apollo's onboard crew were televised. We could sit in our living rooms and literally watch what was happening in space!

Since those days, Wally Schirra has engaged in a variety of civic and humanitarian projects. He serves, presently, on the international board of "Up With People."

Born in Hackensack, New Jersey, Wally is the son of Walter and Florence Schirra. Although no photo of his dad was available, Wally's letter reveals how much he admired the elder Walter, a "World War I flying ace." The following photo is of Wally.

Dear Dad,

I was recalling my first flight, ever, the other day. The World War I ace, my Dad, was flying me, his passenger, then age 13, on a windy day at Teterboro Airport, New Jersey. We took off in that little Aeronca C-3, climbed higher into very strong headwinds, and we were carried backwards across the field boundary! You cleverly lowered the nose and descended into lighter winds and we approached the field again and landed.

To think, that you lived to see me travel into space three times at 13,000 miles per hour.

Your loving Son,
Wally

Phyllis Schlafly

In a note accompanying this photo of her dad, John Bruce Stewart, Phyllis Schlafly told me this was "a typical pose—working on his invention, a rotary gasoline engine." Inventiveness and industry were virtues prized in the St. Louis home of John and Odele Stewart, for daughter Phyllis has become an attorney, author, syndicated columnist, radio commentator, and president of the national organization, Eagle Forum. Named annually by *Good Housekeeping* as one of the "Ten Most Admired Women in the World," her monthly newsletter, "The Phyllis Schlafly Report," is now in its twentieth year.

Recently, President Reagan appointed her as a member of the Commission on the Bicentennial of the U.S. Constitution.

Somehow, Phyllis has also found time to raise a family of six children and to write a dozen books. Her works include *A Choice Not an Echo, The Power of the Positive Woman, Kissinger on the Couch*, and *Child Abuse in the Classroom*. Her radio commentaries on politics and social issues are heard on 200 stations coast to coast, and she has given testimony before more than 50 congressional and state legislative committees. There is very little grass indeed growing under this lady's feet! That is her photo next to her father.

117

Dear Dad:

Thank you for your love and encouragement for everything I ever did and wanted. Thank you for always saying that whatever I did was perfect (even though it wasn't). Thank you for never finding fault, for never second-guessing me, for never putting me down. Thank you for being a role-model of industriousness, perseverance, patience, and cheerfulness. Thank you for the constancy of emotional support you gave me at every age, for every challenge, with every project. Thank you for your lifetime of fidelity to home and hearth, to the faith of our fathers living still, and for giving me an emotional security that transcended disappointments, defeats, and economic reverses.

Love,
Phyllis

William E. Simon

Maybe you're like me—money disappears from my hands so fast I hardly ever notice whose face is on the bill or, still less, whose signature is found above the engraved title "Secretary of the Treasury"! But if you were watching your money closely between 1974 and 1977, you may have seen the name "William E. Simon" written above that title. During those years, Simon served as the 63rd U.S. Secretary of the Treasury, a post first held by Alexander Hamilton.

He has also served as the first Administrator of the Federal Energy Office, as well as Chairman of the East-West Trade Board. Currently, he chairs President Reagan's Productivity Commission and is a member of his Economic Policy Advisory Board. Besides these governmental responsibilities, Simon is currently Chairman, Board of Trustees, of the newly created U.S. Olympic Foundation. And like so many of the personalities whose letters are in this book, Simon is also an author. His books *A Time For Truth* and *A Time for Action* have both been best sellers.

The son of Charles and Eleanor Simon, Bill was born in Paterson, New Jersey. He regrets that no photo of his dad, who died in 1964, was available. The following photo is of Bill.

Dear Dad:

Although it doesn't seem possible, it has been twenty-four years since your death. So much has happened to me in that time that I want to tell you of.

Two months after you left us in June of 1964 I was made partner at Salomon Brothers. You better than anyone would have taken a special pleasure in that, Dad, and in the successes I have had the good fortune to know since. In all the years that followed—from my time in government under Presidents Nixon and Ford, to my various business accomplishments, to my tenure as President of the U.S. Olympic Committee in the year of the Olympics in Los Angeles—I have often thought of you and pictured you as a spectator to it all. With each of the seven children in my family came another moment in which I thought you would be pleased.

Each of my successes would have been so much sweeter had you been there to share them with me— and that much more meaningful in the sharing. I had always hoped that when my ship came in, I would be able to repay you for all of the support and sacrifice and love you gave me.

Let's just say that I welcome an opportunity to say some of the things that I have been thinking since

1964. For all my happy moments in life, I am indebted to you. For all of the love you gave me and the encouragement you showed when I most needed it, I thank you. For all the sacrifices you made for your children and the joy you took in doing so, I salute you. And for simply giving me the life you so helped me to value and enjoy, you have my eternal love.

Your son,
Bill

John C. Swayze

He likes chili, onions, garlic, Dixieland, and he is a tap dancing buff. He used to make the best dressed lists and gained a reputation for his ties. One night when he missed appearing on a TV program, a viewer sent him this wire: "Next time you can't come, send your tie."

Such is the colorful world of John Cameron Swayze. I remember as a youngster being a part of that world, night after night, as I watched Swayze anchor the NBC "News Caravan," one of the two first network television news programs. In addition, John has narrated and hosted several travel programs, one of them, "Sightseeing with the Swayzes," featuring his wife, son and daughter as they traveled about the United States.

Born in Wichita, Kansas, Swayze got the first two-thirds of his catchy name at the last minute, as his parents carried him to the Second Presbyterian Church in Kansas City on a blistering hot day. Swayze, senior, suddenly turned to his wife Mary and said, "We'll name him after your father." That was John Cameron of Scotland. John Cameron Swayze's dad, Jesse, is pictured in the elegantly formal photo on the next page, along with a photo of John.

124

Dear Dad:

There are a lot of things I could have told you when you were here and I wish I had. Just now, when I sat down and thought about it I realized they could be summed up this way. You were not only a 110% man, one who loved to fish and hunt, who had a great stock of energy that you put into your work with success, who liked people but didn't care for windy characters or undue quibbling or liars, who liked dealing on the up and up in life. You were a gentleman. I remember you with pride and affection and, believe me, I know how lucky I was to have you and Mother as parents.

I'll be seeing you again one of these days and it will be a happy occasion for me. Until then, I am,

Your grateful son,
John

John Travolta

"Man, nobody pushed me into show business. I was aching for it," says John Travolta. It was an ache that paid off: by the time he was a mere 23, John had become cinema's hottest, newest superstar, with the release of the disco music film *Saturday Night Fever* (1977). Travolta was named the year's best actor by the National Board of Review and received an Oscar nomination.

There followed quickly two more hugely popular hits, the film version of *Grease* (with Olivia Newton-John), and *Urban Cowboy.* Travolta recreated the role of Tony in the "Fever" sequel *Staying Alive,* which was directed by Sylvester Stallone.

For the last several years, John Travolta has lived on a 17 acre ranch in Santa Barbara, California. Since his hobby is flying, he gets around by piloting his own $1.7 million dollar jet! John was born to Salvatore and Helen Travolta in Englewood, New Jersey. John Travolta's father—shown being hugged in the photo on the right—received the letter which follows three years ago, shortly before Father's Day.

A Premature Father's Day Message for You,

I must tell you, in case you don't already know, one, how much I love you and two, what an incredible upbringing you gave me. If you think about it, I had everything I needed emotionally and materially. You always spent the maximum time you could with me—talking, building, sharing thoughts, desires and ambitions. Think of the kind of lifestyle you afforded us, a pool every year, two vacations, barbecues every night in the summer, a nightclub in our basement, freedom and trust to come and go as we pleased, complete confidence in our creative and athletic abilities, a sense of humor, open house for our friends with enough food to feed the neighborhood, money to buy the latest fashion in clothing, any book we wanted or movie we wanted to see, Christmas that didn't stop, toys galore, always something to look forward to, whether it was building a go-cart, a plane, a bar, a fence, barbecue, basement, attic, garage, fairs for the neighborhood with actual rides for them to enjoy, like the rollercoaster you bought me from Sterns or the go-cart you also bought at Sterns and we made into another elaborate ride that we built together.

When we could take our vacations, Joey and I would get what seemed like unlimited amounts of money for rides, food, and games at the amusement park. The time we spent alone on a fantasy airplane, if that wasn't enough already, I don't know what is. Your sense of responsibility toward your family is probably the best I've ever seen. So thank you for your love, affection, and your everlasting support and interest in your family's life. Again, that alone would have been enough to get us by, but you gave much more to all of us. It's no wonder I have such an unending love toward our family. That was all we were ever taught from the beginning.

So if you ever doubt your contribution, as a provider for your family in every way, you're wasting your time.

Dad, you couldn't have done it better. You're actually pretty amazing especially because I'm fully aware of the demanding brat I was. Your tolerance for me was incredible. Thank you again for taking such good care of us all. You're a great father, a loving person, and I will never not appreciate everything you've done. Especially, your helping me make my dreams come true. I couldn't ask for more.

Love,
Your son John

John Weitz

"The modern man must never look as if he is of any specific nationality. The jet plane has wiped away all of those differences. Modern clothes must be featherweight, easy to pack . . . Most of all a man must always look fit and scrubbed, and he should wear his clothes as if they are old and valued friends." Such is the fashion philosophy of John Weitz, one of a handful of men who created the modern concept of "men's fashions." Weitz has become the premiere name in American menswear, on both sides of the Atlantic and in Japan.

Mr. Weitz divides his working year between New York, London and Tokyo, though he considers New York his home. During the 1950s he was an internationally licensed amateur race driver. He was one of the first men to appear on the International Best Dressed List (1967), and in 1971 was voted to its permanent Hall of Fame. Weitz is married to former actress Susan Kohner, an Academy Award nominee and winner of two Golden Globe Awards.

In addition to his passion for fashion and racing, John Weitz the novelist is author of best sellers like *The Value of Nothing* and *Friends in High Places*. The son of Robert and Hedy Weitz, John was born in Berlin. Perhaps his dad, pictured foreground on the next page as an elegant equestrian, inspired John's love for the finer things of life! The other photo is of John himself.

Dear Dad,

I know I was an expensive son. All those private schools and all those vacation trips and all those special instructors like the ski teacher and the sailing master and heaven-knows-what-else. But Dad, dear Dad, *you* turned out to be an expensive father.

After all, it was you who taught me the art of staying in good hotels, eating in good restaurants, flying first class, wearing expensive clothes, driving expensive cars, and sending my kids to those same expensive Boarding Schools.

Perhaps that is a good thing. After all, pressure makes one perform.

Now that I am at the exact age you were when last I saw you, let's have a brotherly drink. From one spoiled old fellow to another: salud!

See you later.

Love,
John

Michael Westmore

If you saw *Mask, Rocky (I, II,* or *III!), Raging Bull, Clan of the Cave Bear, Flower Drum Song*, or any of dozens of other films or TV specials (e.g., "Eleanor and Franklin"), then you were looking at the make-up art of Michael Westmore. His work in *Mask* (1986) was honored with the Academy Award for "Best Achievement in Make-up," while his artistry in "Eleanor and Franklin" (1976), "Why Me?" (1984), and "Three Wishes of Bill Grier" (1985), all received Emmy Awards.

A graduate of the University of California at Santa Barbara, Michael Westmore has also devoted his time and talent to research in the field of therapeutic cosmetics.

Westmore's make-up book, *The Art of Theatrical Makeup for Stage and Screen* has become a virtual classic, and his how-to video, *Looking Your Best: Secrets of the Hollywood Stars*, is also very popular.

Michael was born in Hollywood to parents Monty and Edith Westmore. His dad, pictured in the white suit, died when Michael was only 18 months old, a fact that lends special poignancy to the letter that follows.

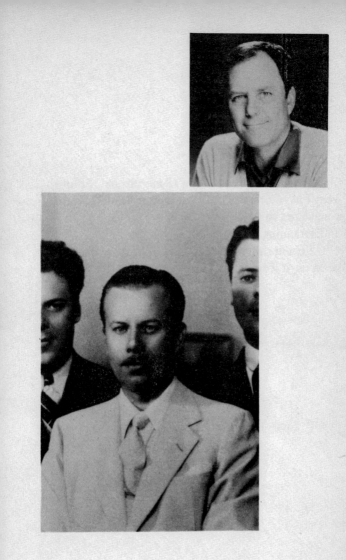

135

Dear Dad,

You died when I was only 18 months old. From what I have heard about you, Dad, I would have very much liked to have grown up with your care, understanding and love.

If I could shout only one message across the heavens, it would be, "until then, I love you."

Michael

Betty White

Remember Sue Ann Nivens on TV's "The Mary Tyler Moore Show"? That was Betty White. And now, of course, she's famous for her role in "Golden Girls." She's received Emmys for both those roles. A perennially popular talk-show guest, she has been seen often on "The Tonight Show," "The Merv Griffin Show," and many others. Betty got her start in roles on such successful radio series as "Blondie," "The Great Gildersleeve," and "This is Your FBI." (Remember those?) In 1949, she joined a local Los Angeles television program which was broadcast daily for five hours. Eddie Albert was with her on the show, but when Albert left to make a film, Betty took over the show, doing it all by herself for 32 ½ hours weekly, for three years. That *has* to be some kind of record for endurance in televison history!

Betty White's pioneering contributions to TV comedy were recognized as early as 1952, when she won an Emmy for the syndicated sit-com, "Life With Elizabeth." She now lives in the Brentwood area of Los Angeles with her two dogs and a black cat, though she was born in Oak Park, Illinois, to Horace and Tess White. Her love of animals was inspired in large measure by her dad, who is pictured (along with Betty and a favorite pet) in the photo on the next page.

Dearest Dad,

Every time someone asks me how I came by my deep love for animals, I smile. Being your daughter, how could I miss?

My most treasured memories are our pack trips into the High Sierras. You and Mom tying me on to dear old reliable Queenie's saddle when I got big enough to ride alone. But remember, the *first* trip when I was two and a half and rode with you holding me in front of you? It took us two days to pack in then—over Kearsarge Pass, Glenn Pass, Baxter Pass. It was all magic country—pure and breathtaking. Today, Daddy, crowds of people drive in to their condominium villages where our wildflower meadows and secret fishing holes used to be. Because of you, however, those places still exist for me, crystal-clear, and I can almost draw every rock and tree, magpie and chipmunk. When things get rough sometimes, I run to that mental high country—and it helps.

> Thank you, darling
> All my love,
> Bets

PART
TWO

Some Thoughts
About Fathers

The richness of the letters I received for the *Dear Dad* project inspired me to look for other stories about fathers and their children, and about the feelings that are part of that relationship. Searching through many dozens of biographies and autobiographies, novels and poems, I began to sense that a single question ran through the memories and reflections of children about their fathers: Who are these men, our fathers? Who are they? When we're very young, they seem so big, so far away—so *foreign*. And that image persists for a long while, until one day we recognize that they are only regular-sized people (maybe even a little on the small side), with faults and fears of their own. For a while, the mystery goes away.

But later it comes back. The older we grow, it seems, the more we realize that our fathers can never be *just* other people. Even if we are friends with them, they are not like our other friends. They are our fathers, and that will never change. The mystery of their private world, of our own beginnings, will always be there.

We try for the rest of our lives to make a place in the imagination for our fathers to occupy. Whether our fathers are alive or dead, whether we ever knew them or not, loved them or not, still we have to make a place for them, and learn how to think about them.

The works I looked at held many stories, far more than I could include here. So I've selected a few that seem to describe especially well some of the many places which people have made for the images of father, and gathered them together with some of my own "thoughts about fathers."

LNC

It seems to me that the memories of our fathers which remain the clearest and most affecting are very often about small incidents that seemed enormous to a young, vulnerable child.

[James] Jones still cared for his father, however, for Ramon Jones read books and continued to try to write poetry. He was also proud and grateful for the support his father gave him. Jones once pushed another boy through the large plate glass window of a store and, afraid of the consequences, ran directly to a nearby bowling alley, where he knew he could find his father. He told him what had happened, and, even though "he was half tight, he got right up and went back across the street with me and took the whole thing on his shoulders and got it straightened out. I'll never forget that. It's a fine thing for a boy to have someone who is rather like a rock to his small intellect, someone who will always be there when needed."

Frank MacShane,
*Into Eternity:
The Life of James Jones*

I have a sense, and perhaps you do too, that while mothers often become symbols of "home," fathers become the "going home."

Home before dark. My father liked to tell the story about my younger brother Fred. When Fred was a little boy, we lived in a small house on a big estate called Beechwood, in Scarborough, New York, about twenty-five miles up the Hudson River from New York City. Once, at twilight after a long summer day, my father was standing outside the house under the big elm tree that shaded the flagstones in front of the door. Fred came back from playing with some friends, worn out and tired too, and when he saw Daddy standing there he ran across the grass and threw his little boy's body into his father's arms.

"I want to go home, Daddy," he said, "I want to go home." Of course he *was* home, just a few feet from the front door in fact. But that didn't make any difference, as my father well understood. We all want to go home, he would say when he told this story. We all do.

Susan Cheever,
*Home Before Dark:
A Biographical Memoir
of John Cheever*

As in this, a favorite book of mine, the whole spectrum of intense emotions is present in the relationship between father and child. Sometimes, the memories settle at one end of the spectrum—or the other.

I was a shy, solemn child even at the age of two, and I am sure that even when I danced I never smiled. My earliest recollections are of being dressed up and allowed to come down to dance for a group of gentlemen who applauded and laughed as I pirouetted before them. Finally, my father would pick me up and hold me high in the air. He dominated my life as long as he lived, and was the love of my life for many years after he died.

Eleanor Roosevelt,
*The Autobiography of
Eleanor Roosevelt*

Reading Mark Twain, I found this evidence of a frontier father.

My father and I were always on the most distant terms when I was a boy—a sort of armed neutrality, so to speak. At irregular intervals this neutrality was broken, and suffering ensued; but I will be candid enough to say that the breaking and suffering were always divided with strict impartiality between us—which is to say, my father did the breaking and I did the suffering.

Mark Twain,
Quoted in *Mark Twain at Your Fingertips*,
Edited by Caroline T. Harnsberger

I've come to the conclusion that there is no one *good way of fathering. Some fathers make their deepest impressions through a manner of gentleness, a habit of interest, a touch...*

I do not believe he ever spoke an angry word to any of his children in his life; but I am certain that it never entered our heads to disobey him. I well remember one occasion when my father reproved me for a piece of carelessness; and I can still recall the feeling of depression which came over me, and the care which he took to disperse it by speaking to me soon afterwards with especial kindness. He kept up his delightful, affectionate manner towards us all his life. I sometimes wonder that he could do so, with such an undemonstrative race as we are; but I hope he knew how much we delighted in his loving words and manner. How often, when a man, I have wished when my father was behind my chair, that he would pass his hand over my hair, as he used to do when I was a boy.

Francis Darwin,
*The Life and Letters
of Charles Darwin*

*What would it be like, I've wondered, to share a very
human father with the whole world?*

But I did know my father. I knew that he listened
carefully when I talked with him and that he answered
my questions thoughtfully. He wasn't like most grown-
ups, who would sort of half listen just long enough to
catch the gist of what you were saying and then bore
you to death with advice. My father asked questions.
And he touched. He would brush at my hair with his
fingertips while he was thinking aloud or while I was
telling him what I thought. He'd put down what he was
doing when I spoke to him, and he'd turn those fantas-
tic brown eyes and that smile toward me and the whole
room would light up. I'd feel that I was the only person in the world who mattered to him. Later, when I
learned that he made almost everyone he liked even a
little that way, I didn't really mind. I didn't mind that
he made other people feel special too.

Leatrice Gilbert Fountain,
*Dark Star: The Untold Story
Of the Meteoric Rise and
Fall of the Legendary
John Gilbert*

Other fathers seem to show love through the action of their lives.

I think of him as being very affectionate, but I don't remember him putting his arm around me. You always had the sense that he had great feeling for you. You saw him providing for you, at enormous pain to himself. You saw him doing nothing for himself—never bought himself anything, never enjoyed himself . . . So the overwhelming impression we got was that this man was offering us his life: he didn't have to put his arm around you.

Mario Cuomo,
as reported in
"Profiles: Governor Mario
Cuomo," *by* Ken Auletta,
in The New Yorker

I've found that dipping into a great writer's memories is one good way to see how others view their fathers.

Pop was a golden man living in a golden age, doing it well, and barely realizing that he was dumping six kids into an age of terror and destruction. I think at the end he worried a bit about this, and he did not underestimate either the meaning or the damage of the First War; but I'm glad he died before the real carnage began—not because he wouldn't have had the character to stand up to it but because it would have destroyed the pattern that you and I like to remember, and that he fitted so beautifully.

It is hard to know, precisely, what a parent transmits to a child, and I have often wondered—not only about what I received from Father but about what I handed along to Joe. Pop was not only conservative (in a rather sensible and large-spirited way) but he was tidy in large and small ways, and I think those are the traits that found their way into the second generation. I can see it in my work. I don't always like it, but I can usually see it. I don't know whether a passionate love of the natural world can be transmitted or not, but like

the love of beauty it is a thing one likes to associate
with the scheme of inheritance.

Letters of E.B. White,
Edited and collected by
Dorothy Lobrano Guth

Perhaps you've come to believe, as I have, that difficult, complex, even unhappy fathers can leave their children with an awareness of being loved and guided—although in unexpected ways.

I cannot remember having ever heard a single sentence uttered by my mother in the nature of moral or religious instruction. My father made an effort or two. When he caught me imitating him by pretending to smoke a toy pipe he advised me very earnestly never to follow his example in any way; and his sincerity so impressed me that to this day I have never smoked, never shaved, and never used alcoholic stimulants. He taught me to regard him as an unsuccessful man with many undesirable habits, as a warning and not as a model. In fact he did himself some injustice lest I should grow up like him; and I now see that this anxiety on his part was admirable and lovable; and that he was really just what he so carefully strove not to be: that is, a model father.

Shaw, *An Autobiography: 1856-1898*,
Edited by Stanley Weintraub

Isn't this a touching story of John Steinbeck about his father?

I remember his restlessness. It sometimes filled the house to a howling although he did not speak often. He was a singularly silent man—first I suppose because he had few words and second because he had no one to say them to. He was strong rather than profound...I often wonder about him. In my struggle to be a writer, it was he who supported and backed me and explained me—not my mother. She wanted me desperately to be something decent like a banker. She would have liked me to be a successful writer like Tarkington but this she didn't believe I could do. But my father wanted me to be myself. Isn't that odd. He admired anyone who laid down his line and followed it undeflected to the end. I think this was because he abandoned his star in little duties and let his head go under in the swirl of family, money and responsibility. To be anything pure requires an arrogance he did not have, and a selfishness he could not bring himself to assume. He was a man intensely disappointed in himself. And I think he liked the complete ruthlessness of my design to be a writer in spite of mother and hell.

Jackson J. Benson,
*The True Adventures of
John Steinbeck, Writer*

While still very young, Truman Capote sent an emotional message to his father after returning from a Christmas visit with him. As Truman was being driven to the bus station in a taxi with his father, his father frantically asked him to tell him that he loved him. Truman couldn't say it. This haunted him on his long trip home to his mother's house. He longed to be with his elderly cousin, Sook, who soothed him and helped him to make everything right:

. . . Stars sparkled, snow whirled inside my head; the last thing I remembered was the peaceful voice of the Lord telling me something I must do. And the next day I did it. I went with Sook to the post office and bought a penny postcard. That same postcard exists today. It was found in my father's safety deposit box when he died last year. Here is what I had written him: *Hello pop hope you are well I am and I am lurning to pedel my plain so fast I will soon be in the sky so keep your eyes open and yes I love you Buddy.*

Truman Capote,
One Christmas

What do you suppose Stevenson's dad thought when he got this letter?

After his father's Paris visit, Louis wrote him a rather odd letter, part of which runs: "I have taken a step towards more intimate relations with you. But don't expect too much of me. This is a rare moment and I have profited by it; but take it as a rare moment."

James Pope Hennessy,
Robert Louis Stevenson

Have you noticed that sometimes, the passage of years is the only thing which can bring things to rightness between father and child?

. . . her father stayed in her house until his death at eighty. . .

"I learned at last to know him and to value him as man, as scholar, as saint. He lived in my house all those years, a gentleman distinguished and learned. We came into a new relationship, a friendship, with mutual respect and affection."

Theodore F. Harris,
Pearl S. Buck,
A Biography

I loved this passage from a Long Island neighbor of mine.

If he had died earlier, especially at the time of my divorce, there would have been something unresolved between us, some canker in my feelings about him. But now we'd had our talk out—not specifically about our differences (we were a reticent pair who just happened to talk a lot), but in such a way that the differences dwindled to nothing. Touchingly, he sometimes seemed almost to defer to me as if I, being in the thick of life, was now the person to consult. But above all there was a great sweetness felt by everyone he met, now that the battles were well and truly over, and serene, uncluttered, uncritical love of his myriad friends and his family.

Wilfrid Sheed,
Frank and Maisie:
A Memoir with Parents

Sometimes, I've grown to suspect, the distance just can't be closed, and death only finalizes the separation.

In late 1850 Lincoln's father lay dying in a farmhouse in Coles County. John Johnston—Sally's boy—wrote Lincoln semiliterate letters about Thomas's condition, saying he would not recover and wondering why Lincoln refused to reply. "Because," Lincoln, finally informed Johnston in January, 1851, "it appeared to me I could write nothing which could do any good." And Lincoln couldn't visit his father either, since Mary was ill and he had pressing business commitments. But he did send a final message to the dying man, to that father who was a stranger to him, who perhaps hadn't been positive and close and understanding and intelligent enough in raising his only son. "Tell him," Lincoln wrote Johnston, "to remember to call upon, and confide in, our great, and good, and merciful Maker; who will not turn away from him in any extremity. He notes the fall of a sparrow, and numbers the hairs of our heads; and He will not forget the dying man, who puts his trust in Him. Say to him that if we would meet now, it is doubtful whether it would not be more painful than pleasant; but that if it be his lot to go now, he will soon have a joyous [meeting] with many loved ones gone before; and where [the rest] of us, through the help of God, hope erelong [to join] them."

On January 17, 1851, Thomas Lincoln died.

Stephen B. Oates,
With Malice Toward None:
The Life of Abraham Lincoln

No matter what the relationship was like in life, the death of the father strikes every child to the heart, as Freud knew.

Within little more than a week, the feelings that made his self-analysis so necessary were coming to the surface. "By one of the obscure routes behind the official consciousness the old man's death affected me deeply," he wrote on November 2, 1896. "I valued him highly and understood him very well indeed, and with his peculiar mixture of deep wisdom and imaginative light-heartedness he meant a great deal in my life. By the time he died his life had long been over, but at a death the whole past stirs within one."

"I feel now as if I had been torn up by the roots."

Ronald W. Clark,
*Freud, The Man
And the Cause*

Sometimes, the death of a father can arouse painful feelings of guilt and self-accusation.

My father had an extraordinary affection for me. He was the silliest man I ever knew and yet cruelly shrewd. He thought and talked of me up to his last breath. I was very fond of him always, being a sinner myself, and even liked his faults. Hundreds of pages and scores of characters in my books came from him. His dry (or rather wet) wit and his expression of face convulsed me often with laughter. He kept it in his old age . . .

I knew he was old. But I thought he would live longer. It is not his death that crushed me so much but self-accusation.

*Selected Letters of
James Joyce,*
Edited by Richard Ellman

As Jack Lemmon notes, the process of sorting out our feelings for our fathers goes on throughout life, and is never completed.

. . . I know that my feelings about my father were an important drive in my life—a good drive, I think. I always loved him very much but it's difficult to differentiate, when you're young, between real love and duty and respect, a feeling of obligation. For me it was a peculiar combination, trying to be "on" and prove, and also being reticent and afraid I could never—you know—satisfy my father or satisfy other people that I could be on a level with him. I guess the only thing that's important is that he *was* my father. He was some guy, my Dad was. Some guy.

Don Widener,
Lemmon, A Biography

I couldn't agree more with what Gloria Swanson says in the following passage: no relationship—even the one with our fathers—can ever be complete.

But Daddy was the most complicated figure in my life, probably. I had adored him until I was fifteen, and then had felt for him a mixture of love and pity during the nine years since. I had somehow tried to replace him with the two men I had married, but without success, for in my grief I knew that for me he had always been a full presence, a total reality, someone different from everyone else, someone no one could ever replace. If our relationship had been incomplete, then perhaps it was time I understood that all relationships are incomplete to some extent. No two people can ever know each other completely. My father's life had been his to live. He had made all his own choices. I had no right, as another person, even as his only daughter, to question the choices he had made, just as I felt no one had any right ultimately to question my choices regarding my own life.

Gloria Swanson,
Swanson On Swanson

And so, I believe, our fathers are mysteries that continue to live in us.

Pat went down quietly to his father and sat beside him on the steps, huddling close to the great arched back, the huge hairy arms of him. —And oh, the pain to reach, to touch, to know him, this giant of a man, his father, puffing contentedly on the battered pipe. They sat the two thus silently until the paleness in the sky bled slowly into the dusk, till yellow-gold spatters of light flicked on across the valley.

Michael O'Malley,
Miners Hill

Our fathers are lost to us, and we to them. We spend our lives trying to find each other.

My friend, this body offers to carry us for nothing —as the ocean carries logs. So on some days the body wails with its great energy; it smashes up the boulders, lifting small crabs, that flow around the sides.

Someone knocks on the door. We do not have time to dress. He wants us to go with him through the blowing and rainy streets, to the dark house.

We will go there, the body says, and there find the father whom we have never met, who wandered out in a snowstorm the night we were born, and who then lost his memory, and has lived since longing for his child, whom he saw only once . . . while he worked as a shoemaker, as a cattle herder in Australia, as a restaurant cook who painted at night.

When you light the lamp you will see him. He sits there behind the door . . . the eyebrows so heavy, the forehead so light . . . lonely in his whole body, waiting for you.

Robert Bly,
Selected Poems

168

Who are our fathers? They are images in memory.

His father came back to him in the fall of the year, or in the early spring when there had been jacksnipe on the prairie, or when he saw shocks of corn, or when he saw a lake, or if he ever saw a horse and buggy, or when he saw, or heard, wild geese, or in a duck blind; or remembering the time an eagle dropped through the whirling snow to strike a canvas-covered decoy, rising, his wings beating, the talons caught in the canvas. His father was with him, suddenly, in deserted orchards and in new-plowed fields, in thickets, on small hills, or when going through dead grass, whenever splitting wood or hauling water, by grist mills, cider mills and dams and always with open fires.

Ernest Hemingway,
"Fathers and Sons," in
Winner Take Nothing

ABOUT THE EDITOR

L. Norma Cox holds a Master's Degree in Education from Antioch University, and has recently retired from her long career in Fund Raising and Public Relations. She now lives in Connecticut with her husband, Joseph Ferlatt, and their two longhaired dachshunds, Shekel and Becky, and is currently at work on her second book.